Power Football

Power

E. P. Dutton & Co., Inc.

New York

Football

Murray Chass
and the Editors of
Pro Quarterback

Library of Congress Cataloging in Publication Data

Chass, Murray.
    Power football.

    1. Football–Biography.   I. Pro quarterback.   II. Title.
GV939.A1C46   796.33′2′0922   73-79542
ISBN 0-525-18255-1

Contents

What Is Power Football

If a little old woodcarver from the tiny European country of Liechtenstein were suddenly plunked down in Kansas City's Arrowhead Stadium one autumn Sunday afternoon in the most heated moments of a game between the Chiefs and the Oakland Raiders, he very likely would think he was intruding on (1) the last battle of the Vietnam war (2) a fight to the death between two savage jungle tribes or (3) a clash between gladiators and lions left over from the days of the Colosseum in Rome.

No, a kindly native would explain, this is professional football, a sport indigenous to the United States. Sport! the little old woodcarver would repeat in astonishment; as a sport, this would make a good barbaric rite indigenous to the fiercest head hunters of deepest Africa. It would even rival driving on the Los Angeles freeways on a tricycle.

It wouldn't be surprising for the Liechtensteinian to react that way because people who watch the game 20 or 25 Sundays every year and those who play it often think of the game that way, emphasizing the brutality and the violence. Pro football physicians especially are aware of the brutality because they are charged with the responsibility of getting the victims of the violence healthy before they miss too many skirmishes.

"These players are gladiators; they really are," says Dr. Thomas Shindler, orthopedic surgeon of the Houston Oilers. "They like it. They want to play. They ask to play. If they're injured, they want to get back in. These people are a special breed. These fellows enjoy this direct confrontation. They play with pain every Sunday."

Jets' Al Atkinson and J. W. Hicks crunch ball carrier.

If, however, that pain becomes too excruciating because it emanates from torn knee ligaments or a ruptured Achilles tendon, emergency action sometimes is called for.

"It's like being in Vietnam," Dr. James Nicholas, the curator of Joe Namath's knees, once said. "There's immediate evacuation to the hospital, immediate admission to the hospital, immediate setting up of the operating room, immediate examination and immediate surgery."

The brutality cannot be denied. However, a glance below the surface of the obvious force of the physical contact inherent in the game reveals another kind of power, a power that is just as integral a part of the sport

Emerson Boozer of Jets takes blow to jaw.

and one that is even more vital. That power is found in the artistry of the game—the long pass that takes a team out of a hole, the short pass that gets the crucial first down, the burst through the middle for a touchdown, the slashing slant off tackle that goes for a sizeable gain, the flowing sweep that sets up the winning touchdown, the jarring tackle that stops the runner behind the line, the pass interception by the same man who deftly back-pedals into his team's zone pass coverage.

Thus, Joe Namath's right arm represents power. Larry Csonka's oak-like legs are power. The shrewd minds of John Unitas and Bob Griese that keep a defense off balance and an offense driving—that's power, too. So is the forearm of Dick Butkus and the bear-like tackle of Willie Lanier.

In reality, the power actually begins in the minds of two men—the quarterback and the middle linebacker. The quarterback uses his knowledge of the defense and of what's working with his offense this particular day to produce a play that will gain yardage, either for a first down or a touchdown. The middle linebacker, on the other hand, generally serves as the quarterback of the defense and uses his knowledge and his instinct to try and frustrate the offensive quarterback's strategy. A game, therefore, is a constant mental struggle between these two men to see who can outguess whom and foil the other's plans.

There are, of course, other attributes the quarterback and the middle linebacker must have.

As far as quarterbacks are concerned, John Hadl points out that anyone who comes into the National Football League can throw the football.

"The difference is in how much a man wants to compete," the Los Angeles quarterback says. "I mean the ability to stand in there and take a chance on a beating by some big defensive lineman until the right time comes to let go of the ball. Passing is timing. Nothing is more important except releasing the ball at exactly the right instant.

"Therefore, accuracy means less than guts. You know where your receiver is going to be because you've practiced it a hundred times. I also know how much I've got to put on the ball. The only variable is in my stomach. The only question is whether I'm going to feel the rush so much that I'll release the pass before I should. If I do, it's incomplete or worse."

The middle linebacker is the man who makes a quarterback's life harried and peaceless. Besides setting up the defensive alignments, the

Bob Tatarek of Bills engages in one-on-one combat.

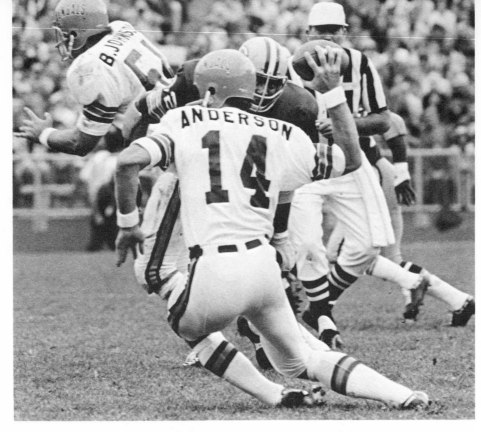

Bengal Ken Anderson tries desperately to pass before going down.

middle linebacker is a ubiquitous urchin, versatile enough to stop the run and break up a pass, not to mention sacking the quarterback occasionally.

"What I like most about playing middle linebacker is the aspect of being involved," says Willie Lanier, Kansas City's brilliant man in the middle. "It's the place on the field where you're involved in basically every running play and to a great extent, most of the passing game as well. It's much easier for the quarterback to throw straight ahead than to each of the sidelines. Consequently, you become involved and I've always enjoyed being a part of every defensive play. Sometimes I feel that regardless of where the ball is and who's carrying it—outside or inside, long pass or what have you—I'm supposed to be near it. You've got to like hitting to be a middle linebacker. If you don't like to hit, you can't play there because you will hit and you will get hit. I've watched some films where a team will send everyone at you.

"There will be situations where I can have the center blocking me for one play, the guard the next time and then tackles and even tight ends get into the act. There are all kinds of combinations that can hit you. So you've got to be ready to deal with it, and it keeps you mentally and physically alert on every play. Even though it may sound contradic-

The flying power of a defensive lineman.

Larry Brown of
the Washington Redskins
tries to hurdle
the Miami line in the
Super Bowl.

This is where it all takes place.

Len Dawson: "We can win it all this season."

Burial ground.

Doug Hart of the Green Bay Packers welcomes Joe Moore of the Chicago Bears.

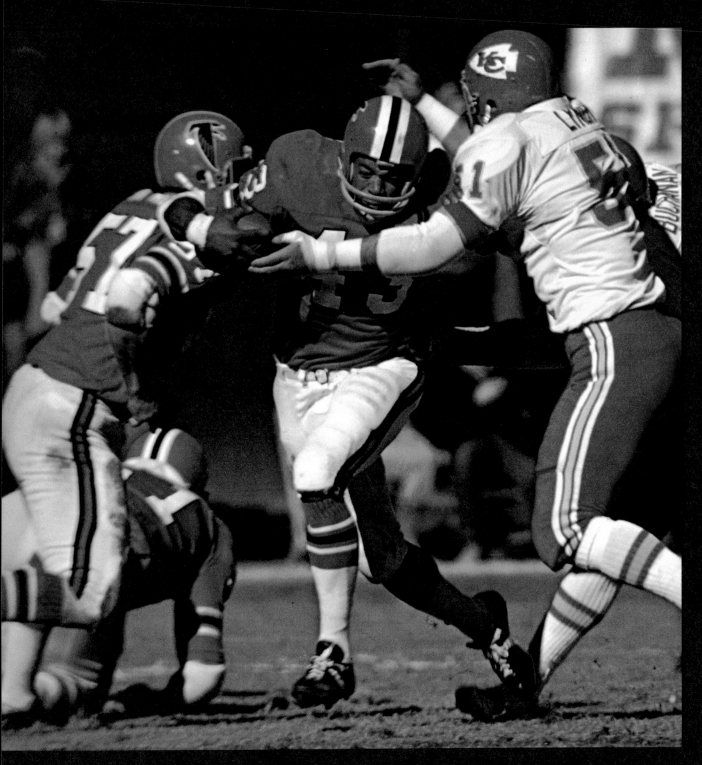

Welcome to the club.

Home at last.

Joe Profit
of the Atlanta Falcons
goes airborne
against New York Jets.

Mike Ditka: Looking for the last man.

Mike Siani: Deception comes both ways.

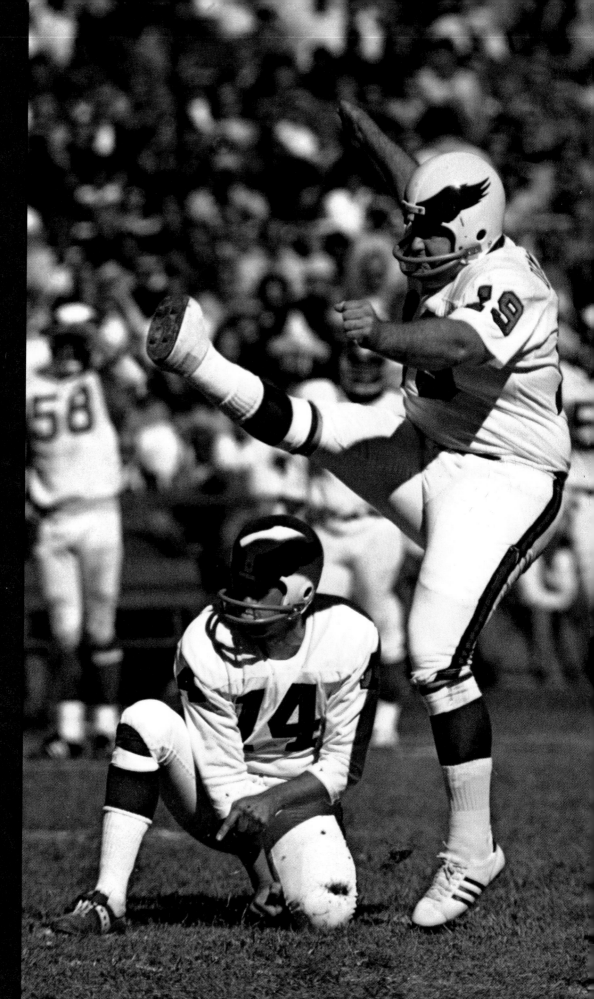

You do it
every way you can.

tory, there are times when you've got to be both cautious and uncautious at the same time. It's a matter of awareness. The nature of the position is such that you must concentrate on every play. If you don't, you can find yourself being physically annihilated."

Running backs face physical annihilation, too, although they're being grown so big these days they can hand out some annihilation of their own.

"When you hit head on, there's no place else for the force to dissipate," says Miami's Larry Csonka. "It's just you and him, and in my case against a defensive back, it's sort of like a Volkswagen hitting a Mack truck."

Early in his pro career, John Brockington found it was to his advantage to run as hard as he could. "Dick Butkus is going to hit you anyway," the Green Bay back says. "And they're not going to get any madder at you if you run harder so you'd best get up in there."

Jets' Clifford McClain grimaces from below.

However, Csonka and Brockington and all the other fine runners in the league haven't amassed their miles of yardage just by running into people and knocking them down. There's much more to being a top-notch running back. For example, Ron Johnson speaks of instinct.

"I don't think you can coach somebody to run with the ball," the New York Giant says. "It's instinct, something you're born with. Oh sure, you can teach a kid how to pick his hole, how to follow his blocking, how to change speeds. But those cuts and fakes and swivels, that's instinct. I don't know how it happens. It's just there."

Running backs were noticeably there during the 1972 NFL season, more noticeably than in any previous season in the league's history. With the defenses becoming more and more sophisticated and therefore harder and harder to pass against, especially the long pass known as the bomb, teams have gone more and more to the running game. This was especially true in 1972 when the league moved the hashmarks closer together, leaving more room on the narrow side of the field.

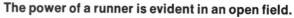

The power of a runner is evident in an open field.

Leroy Kelly of Browns finds the football elusive.

Tight end Ted Kivalick of 49ers leaps for pass.

(Left) Jets' Richard Caster reaches behind for underthrown ball.

(Center) Chargers' Gary Garrison battles for pass with a defensive back.

(Right) Gene Washington of 49ers leaps with defensive back for a high pass.

Offenses took such advantage of the wider area that ten runners gained 1,000 or more yards, a feat never before achieved by more than six runners in one season. In fact, it wasn't until 1959 that the league could boast of ten 1,000-yard rushers in its entire history.

Coaches like to be able to use the run much more than in the past because they are conservative by nature and therefore like their chances of retaining the ball when they keep it on the ground better than when they put it in the air. This is where a brilliant play-calling quarterback, such as Griese or Unitas, can shine because they are masters at ball control football.

Csonka, who is one of the big reasons Griese is so good at controlling the ball, believes coaches and running backs aren't the only ones who like to see the ball stay on the ground.

"Fans today are a lot like people who went to the Colosseum in Rome," he says. "They want brutality, if that's the right word. It's a little hard, but I think brutality fits. They want action. Action equals running and running equals brutality, at least in pro football. You get the big hits, the massive collisions in a running game. You don't get that kind of action passing."

But without the passing, the running would suffer, and vice versa. The quarterback and the running back complement each other in the offensive phase of power football. Then there's the guy on the other side of the line, the middle linebacker, who epitomizes the defensive aspect of the power found in football. When they clash—physically, mentally and artistically—the collision ignites a powerful explosion.

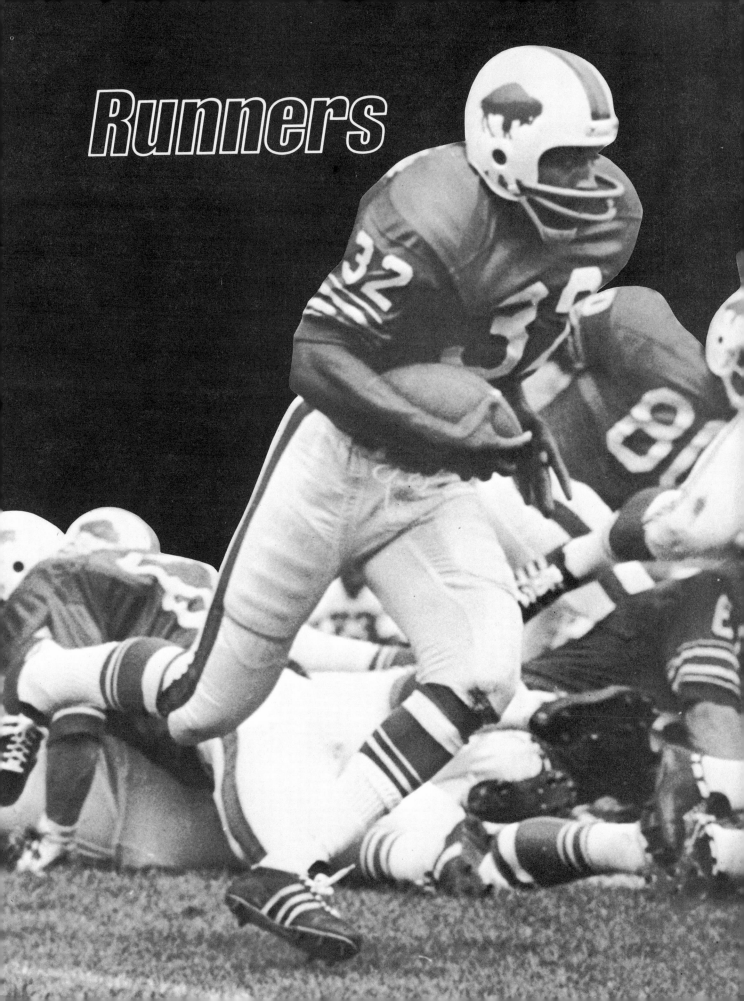

Runners

John Brockington

Boys who are growing up to be 6'1" and 225 pounds aren't supposed to be scared by anything, but John Brockington was scared once during his sophomore year in high school.

"I wasn't a very disciplined football player," recalls Brockington, who built a reputation as a sterling sandlot player before making the team at Thomas Jefferson High in Brooklyn. "I went to practice when I felt like it and if I didn't feel like it, I didn't. If I had something better to do, I did it.

"Well, one day the coach and the two team captains called me in. It was one of the days I was there after I had missed the day before. Coach said he had to let me go because I wasn't helping the team. Man, I'll tell you, I was scared. But then, after a while, he said I could have another chance. I think he was just trying to scare me and he did. I've never missed a practice since then."

Eight years later, when he was fully grown, Brockington was frightened again, but this time in another way. It was just before the start of his sophomore year in the National Football League, and Brockington was thinking about the unexpectedly great success he had as a rookie and also about his unknown future.

"I didn't expect anything like last year and now I just want to be consistent," he said. "Jim Brown beat people because he was there every Sunday, killing them on every play. Mainly, I want that consistency. I don't want to be a one-year flash. It scares me to death, the thought of having one great season and then being an also-ran the rest of my career."

As much chance as there was that John Brockington's high school football coach would have kicked him off the team, that's as much chance that John Brockington had of having one great season and then being an also-ran for the rest of his career.

Brockington had to wait a little longer to find out if he was to be an also-ran than he did to find out he would get a second chance to stay on the high school team, but he found out with certainty.

After establishing a rookie record by gaining 1,105 yards in 1971, Brockington ran for 1,027 yards in 1972 and became the only player in NFL history to rush for 1,000 yards or more in each of his first two seasons. In fact, only six other runners ever have reached the 1,000-yard plateau two years in a row, and one of them, Larry Csonka, did it at the same time Brockington did and he was in his fourth and fifth seasons. The others who have accomplished the feat are Joe Perry, Jimmy Brown, Jim Nance, Leroy Kelly and Jim Taylor.

Taylor, of course, is the big (in both size and success) back against whom all other Packer backs are measured and weighed. He exceeded 1,000 yards for five consecutive seasons, something even Brown never did, and he became a Packer legend.

"But Jim Taylor in his wildest dreams never was as fast as John Brockington," says John (Red) Cochran, offensive backfield coach under Vince Lombardi, who was brought back to the Packers by Dan Devine when he became head coach in 1971. "Taylor was just power, nothing more. He would get caught all the time from behind. He was a great back and he gained lots of yards. You couldn't begin to estimate the yardage he would have had if he'd had speed like Jim Brown—or like Brockington."

The second of three children of a postal worker and his wife, Brockington displayed his size and speed so well in high school that numerous colleges were interested in him. Syracuse, which had developed Jim Brown, Ernie Davis, Jim Nance and Floyd Little, sent him to a prep school, but when it came time to select a college, Brockington and his parents were so impressed with Woody Hayes that he wound up at Ohio State.

There wasn't much, though, that John did in his first two years with the Buckeyes to impress anyone. He started the first two games of his sophomore year as a wingback but then was switched to tailback and was promptly hurt. As a junior, he was given his choice of positions and he chose fullback, then wound up sitting behind Jim Otis all season. "It was a frustrating year," he recalls. "I felt like I missed a whole year of football."

His senior year, though, was entirely different. He was the No. 1 running back on the team, he led Ohio State into the Rose Bowl and he was high on the draft lists of all the pro teams.

He was especially high on Green Bay's list, but the Packers feared the Chicago Bears would grab him before their turn came. Devine, however, was a resourceful plotter. On draft day he traded quarterback Don Horn to Denver for defensive lineman Alden Roche and a gimmick— the Packers got Denver's higher spot in the first round, which was one pick ahead of the Bears.

"I hadn't even thought about Green Bay," Brockington says. "My first reaction was surprise. I knew they had a lot of good backs and I couldn't figure out why they drafted me. I wasn't happy or disappointed, just surprised." But as far as Devine was concerned, Brockington was "the kind of back we needed to make our offense go." And indeed it went.

Brockington really went in a three-game period in the middle of the season, sloshing through soggy turf for 111 yards in 16 carries against Detroit, amassing 142 yards in 30 tries against Chicago and blitzing Minnesota's seemingly impenetrable defense for 149 yards in 23 attempts.

"Brockington is something else," Bud Grant, the Vikings' coach, said after that exhibition of top-flight running. "Their offensive line does a great job for him, but he did a lot himself. He was running with nothing in front of him and all of a sudden he was outside."

Interestingly, Brockington never got the chance to run outside at

Ohio State and he was delighted to be able to do it in Green Bay. "I always liked to run outside and I knew I could," he says.

With legs churning and knees raised high, the Packer bull gets outside in a hurry, and opposing linebackers and backs face a tricky challenge in getting out there with him and bringing him down once they reach him.

"In the films," says Bill Bergey, a Cincinnati linebacker, "he looked like a slashing type of runner, but he powered you, too. One time I made a grab for him and he was like a big slippery fish."

Ron Smith, a Chicago defensive back, once thought he had the Packer stopped. "I made him commit himself and then I tried to get low on him," Smith relates. "Well, he drove into me with all his 225 pounds and he'd gotten up momentum for 15 yards. Boy, he brings his legs up beautifully. I think he got me in the chest with a leg and it hurt."

No one hurt more than Ken Dyer, a Cincinnati defensive back who made the mistake of lowering his head to make the tackle as Brockington reached him. A knee caught Dyer on the chin, his head snapped back and his career was over. His neck had broken.

"I've always run hard and my knees have been high since I was in high school," Brockington says. "You might as well run fast. You're going to get hit anyway so why not get hit running fast?"

Brockington quickly gained the admiration of his teammates, too. He was a rookie, but they knew he was no ordinary rookie.

"He's as hard a running back as I've ever seen," says guard Bill Lueck. "An arm tackle just won't slow him down at all and the speed he has for his size is just amazing. You get a runner like that and you see him breaking his back, and it's embarrassing if you miss your block, really embarrassing."

The confidence the Packers had in Brockington was vividly pointed out in that game against the Bears, the one in which he gained 142 yards.

The Bears had just tied the contest, 14–14, but a 62-yard kickoff return by Dave Hampton placed the ball at Chicago's 39-yard line with only minutes left. It was too far for a field goal so the Packers had to work the ball closer to the goalposts. They didn't fool around; quarterback Scott Hunter handed the ball to Brockington five straight times, and after the whistle had blown on the fifth play, the Packers had their easy field-goal shot at the 15.

After the whistle had blown on the final game of the season,

Brockington had 1,105 yards on 216 carries, which was distinctly better than Jim Brown's rookie record of 942 yards in 200 tries. Furthermore, Brockington barely missed winning the league rushing title, falling 28 yards short of Floyd Little's total.

"I never expected that kind of year," Brockington admits. "It's hard for a rookie to just make the team. I didn't know anything about a passing game, but I learned something about it. I learned to read my blocks, too, and I learned to watch the defense out of the corner of my eye."

He also learned an important lesson—don't think about goals, such as reaching 1,000 yards.

"The last few weeks I felt a lot of pressure," he says. "When you get close to 1,000 yards, the linemen are all talking about it and you worry about getting hurt before you get it. You worry about disappointing the fans and you worry about disappointing yourself.

"It got so toward the end of the season I was looking back to the line on my way back to the huddle to see what I'd gained. Going into our second game with the Bears, I was close enough to get it and that's the first time my hands ever shook before a game. I tried to put it out of my mind but I couldn't. I blew two audibles at the start of the game. I was listening to the signals, but I was so keyed up I couldn't concentrate. To hell with that."

Once a runner reaches the magic number, of course, he has all the more incentive and desire to get there again. In sports, though, everyone makes a big thing out of the troubles a rookie has in repeating an outstanding year. Somewhere along the line, this difficulty was labeled the sophomore jinx. To Brockington, however, there is no such thing. At least that's the attitude he took as he headed into the 1972 season, a season when everybody would be watching closely to see whether, indeed, he could do as well as he had as a rookie.

"If you're ready to play, if you put everything you have into what you're doing, you shouldn't have to worry about it," Brockington said, "unless you get an injury that's going to slow you up. And injuries can happen any year.

"I think what it really amounts to is getting big-headed after a big rookie year and taking too much for granted, not getting to the holes, missing holes, not pushing enough. But I'm not concerned about the sophomore jinx; I'm not worried about a letdown."

To ensure against a letdown, Brockington worked extra hard, spending his own time, for example, running extra sprints to put himself in even better condition.

"In the course of a game," he explained, "you might get tired. I can't afford to get tired. If I carry the ball twenty times in a game, I can't afford to come back to the huddle breathing hard. Plus it helps me in the fourth quarter."

Everything Brockington did in 1972 helped him reach the level all running backs strive for. He fell short of his rookie total, but his 1,027 yards was nonetheless an achievement of note. His per-carry average slid from 5.1 to 3.7, but that could be attributed to problems the Packers had with injuries on their offensive line. Like all runners, Brockington is well aware that he needs a strong line to open holes for him.

The job of the running back is to get to the hole quickly and to dart through it while it's open. Then he's on his own to pick the course he thinks will get him the extra few yards, the tough yards that the outstanding backs get, the ones that make the difference between an 800-yard year and a 1,000-yard year.

Brockington works hard to get those yards, and his work doesn't go unnoticed by his admiring and appreciative teammates.

"John works very hard and concentrates on his assignments," says Bart Starr, Green Bay's former quarterbacking great who also saw the youngster through the eyes of a coach. "That's one reason he was such an immediate hit with the veterans in his first year. I'm very partial to my old teammate, Jimmy Taylor, because I think he was a complete ballplayer. John is becoming that kind of player."

Larry Brown

Pittsburgh's Hill District sits conspicuously and uneasily on the periphery of the city's downtown section, the area that is known as the Golden

Triangle. Unlike the bright lights and the glittering steel and aluminum of the skyscraper office buildings that dot the Golden Triangle, dreary, dilapidated houses and dirty sidewalks populate the Hill. The Hill District doesn't win any Model Cities awards; nor do its houses attract any citations from *Better Homes and Gardens*. More likely, the Hill qualifies for "Ghetto-of-the-Year Award," or one of its residents staggers away with the "Fight-of-the-Night Prize." Larry Brown grew up in the Hill District.

"I lived in a rough neighborhood and you had to be rough to survive," relates Brown, who survives about twenty-five carries a game for the Washington Redskins. "Everybody you associated with, you had to say the right thing to all the time. One little thing said wrong and you'd get into an argument."

At some high school football games in Pittsburgh's City League, fans don't bother arguing; they just fight, and the fights often escalate into riots. This situation is most apt to crop up when a team from a predominantly black school plays a team from a predominantly white school. The school Brown attended, Schenley High, was black.

"Two neighborhood kids got killed in a rumble after a game," Brown recalls. "I can remember another game where there was a fight in the stands. They got us players out of there as fast as possible, but before we got away altogether they started throwing rocks at the bus."

Little wonder, then, that Larry Brown, the NFL's Player of the Year in 1972, can stand before a group of errant youngsters at the District of Columbia's Receiving Home for Children the day after he has gained 106 or 191 Redskin yards and tell them that they can overcome the obstacles that have been placed haphazardly in their paths. He knows whereof he speaks.

"I can identify with these kids; I know what they're going through," he explains. "Believe me, I know about the pimps and crime and prostitutes and drug addicts."

But avoiding the quicksand of the ghetto wasn't the only stutter-step Brown had to take in running from the darkness of the Hill to the glory of the NFL. Wherever this son of a Pennsylvania Railroad baggage-man tried to travel, roadblocks and pitfalls seemed to spring up in his way. From Schenley High School to Dodge City Junior College to Kansas State University to the Washington Redskins, Brown encountered as many problems as Batman and Robin did in a whole year of television episodes.

But with the same determination that is the hallmark of his style as a running back, Brown overcame these obstacles and today has achieved the status of being mentioned in the same breath as the running back against whom all running backs are measured, Jimmy Brown.

"I always said that Jim Brown was the greatest running back I'd ever seen," says Mike McCormack, who blocked for Jim Brown for six years and later served as an assistant coach at Washington before becoming head coach of the Philadelphia Eagles. "But I don't think anybody has a bigger heart, is a better competitor or plays with more desire or toughness than Larry Brown."

"He's the best because of his determination," Charley Harraway, his running mate, notes. "When Larry has the ball, he has it in for the whole world. He has to conquer the world."

If it hadn't been for Vince Lombardi, who as a football coach accomplished just about every feat except walking on water (no one probably ever challenged him), Brown might never have been in a position to do anything with the world but view it as it passed him by.

After moving from the little Wisconsin town he made famous to the nation's capital, Lombardi lived only long enough to coach the Redskins for one year, but that was the year Brown was a rookie and the man whom Henry Jordan said treated everyone alike—like dogs—left an indelible impression on Brown's mind and a special helmet on his head.

"He changed my whole life," says the No. 1 runner in Redskin history. "I loved the man."

The love, though, stems more from a retrospective viewing than from an on-the-spot feeling.

"When I found out that Coach Lombardi was coming to Washington, I figured I had another madman as coach," Brown relates. "Throughout my career, I had coaches like Vince Lombardi. He was what the kids back home would call a 'real mean mother'."

But after all Brown had been through, neither a madman nor a "mean mother" was about to deter him from his ambition. Brown's problems, aside from his everyday situation on the Hill, began when he rejected the college scholarship offers he received because "my parents had financial difficulties and I thought I should stay home and help them."

Then, by the time he decided the best way he could help was by going to school, all the scholarship offers had been withdrawn. With the help of his high school coach, though, he managed to obtain a scholarship

at Dodge City Junior College, only to learn when he arrived at the Kansas school that a coaching change had taken place and he was told by the new coach that he would have to make the team before he could receive financial assistance.

He made the team and earned his scholarship, just as he did when he moved to Kansas State two years later. But the transfer didn't bring an end to his string of dilemmas because as a junior at Kansas State he was a blocking back and as a senior he was a running back in a pass-oriented offense. In other words, the pro scouts didn't hang around to run piggyback with him all over Big Eight fields.

The Redskins, though, liked the way Brown carried out his assigned tasks, no matter how glamorless, and they drafted him as an eighth-round selection. "We ranked him as the fifteenth best halfback in the nation," says Tim Temerario, the team's director of player personnel. "But our original report on him said he wasn't clever as a runner and he missed holes. We underestimated him as a ball carrier but not as much as the rest of the world."

The Redskins also underestimated their chances of signing Brown. They thought it would be a mere formaltiy, but the 5′11″, 195-pound youngster was reluctant to join the Redskins, preferring instead to go to Canada because Washington and its ghettos seemed too much like the ghetto he had escaped and because he felt his size might hamper him in the NFL. Even Lombardi couldn't get Brown to sign his name on a Washington contract. It took the persuasive tones of a scout, Bob White, a black who lived in a beautiful home in northeast Washington, to induce Brown to give up his idea of heading north. "He told me I could make the club," Brown says. "He made me feel that I could start for them."

In trying to win a spot on the team's forty-man roster, though, it was up to Brown and not Lombardi or White or anyone else. Two particular problems plagued him in that effort—he kept dropping the ball and he was slow in breaking from his set position at the snap of the ball.

Lombardi, however, helped the rookie solve both problems. When Brown kept dropping passes, Lombardi came up to him and handed him a football. "He made me carry it everywhere I went for a week—to church, to restaurants, to my room," Brown recalls. "I stopped having trouble catching passes."

He stopped having trouble with his timing, too, once Lombardi discovered he had a hearing problem. "Coach Lombardi told me I was at least a half count late every time in getting off with the ball," the rugged back explains. "He said the ball was almost always in Sonny Jurgensen's hands before I started to move. I was looking at the ball before the play started."

It was then that Lombardi discovered Brown was nearly deaf in his right ear, a distinct disadvantage for an athlete whose success depends first of all on hearing signals and changes of play at the line of scrimmage. But that dilemma wasn't about to stymie Lombardi. The resourceful coach had a special helmet made for Brown in which a hearing receiver was placed on the right side and a speaker on the left side with connecting wires running over his head.

Someday the first test of the helmet may be as famous as Alexander Graham Bell's initial test of his telephone. Standing about fifteen feet or more from Brown in a room at Kennedy Stadium, Lombardi said, "Larry, can you hear me?"

"Coach," Brown replied to the man he was growing very fond of, "I can always hear you."

From then on, Brown could hear the quarterback's signals, too, and that first year, 1969, he heard his number called frequently. He responded by rushing for 888 yards on 202 carries and catching 34 passes for 302 yards, and it was the start of a brilliant career.

In his second season, at the age of twenty-three, Brown led the league in rushing with 1,125 yards, slipped back to 948 yards in 1971 but then amassed 1,216 yards in 1972 despite missing two games with injuries. Because of those absences, he lost the league rushing championship to O. J. Simpson but he nevertheless became the Redskins' all-time leading rusher and more significantly, he powered the team to the Super Bowl and he became only the third runner in NFL history to accumulate 4,000 yards rushing in his first four seasons. His 4,177 yards surpassed Cookie Gilchrist's 4,010 and trailed only Jim Brown's 5,055. In addition, he ran for 100 or more yards 18 times in his first four seasons.

Although Lombardi wasn't around to see Brown achieve such distinctions, the coach wouldn't have been surprised. For Lombardi, an astute judge of talent, raw or otherwise, spotted something in Brown from the early days in his first Washington training camp.

In Brown's recollection, there was one particular moment when he feels Lombardi became aware of him.

"It happened in a nutcracker drill," Brown relates. "He had two big sandbags squeezing two big linemen together and as Sonny handed me the ball, I blasted by both linemen before they could raise up. Right there, in front of God, Sonny, the two linemen and the two sandbags, Coach Lombardi stopped practice and said, 'Nice going.' It was the most extravagant praise that had come out of him since he took over the Redskins."

But if Brown's success wouldn't be surprising to Lombardi, it certainly has been to Mrs. Lawrence Brown, Sr., mother of Larry and his two brothers. "I thought he would become an artist," she says. "He could look at your face and make a beautiful sketch."

Mrs. Brown actually wasn't too far wrong; her son indeed is an artist, but one who paints pictures with his shifting feet and feinting body as he darts between tacklers and plows over others, determined to make a yard here and a couple yards there. He has painted this picture more and more each year as the Redskins have come to rely on him more and more for the power of their offense.

"He is our offense," Sonny Jurgensen has said. "When you have the greatest back in the league and if you're not running him, you're not using your offense. We have to give the ball to him."

"Larry challenges the ability of his own offensive line," says John Wilbur, a member of that line. "You want to block for him. The thing that makes him so great is that he's mean and tough. He breaks tackles and that gives the other team another chance to hit him. The running back takes the worst beating of anyone on the field and he doesn't care."

Brown takes a beating, but he dishes it out in his own way, too, particularly in the way he frustrates the defense with his elusiveness.

"Larry reminds me a lot of a cat," says Bill Bradley, Philadelphia's excellent safety. "He can get hit while he's in the air or off balance, but he always manages to land on his feet and keep going."

In Brown's mind, he's always going, going toward the goal he has set for himself—not to be another Jim Brown but to be the best runner as Larry Brown.

"For a long time, people kept thinking of me as only an average back," Brown said in a rare outburst after he had devastated the New York Giants with a career-high 191 yards one Sunday in 1972. "Everybody's got a big-back theory, but it's not size. It's heart and determination. Man, I learned to run when I was a small kid in the ghetto. Nobody gave me anything. Everything I got I had to work for and make for myself. I'm still working."

And what a beautiful and powerful piece of work he is.

Larry Csonka

News release: The Bryna Cosmetic Company of Miami announced today its selection of Larry Csonka as "the most beautiful player in the NFL." The firm usually gives an annual trophy to one of its female consultants, but this year its employees voted unanimously to give the award to Csonka, whose nose has been broken ten times.

There are some followers of the career of Larry Csonka who would have considered it more apt if the United States Congress had selected Csonka to receive the Congressional Medal of Honor and a Purple Heart or two.

After all, Csonka has served in combat more often than John Wayne, performed more heroic deeds than Rin Tin Tin and, most significant of all, has suffered more casualties than an entire company of marines.

Evidence: His tenth broken nose. "John Elliott (of the New York Jets) hit me low on the legs and I went straight up in the air. I didn't come down at an angle. I came straight down like a B-52 and hit right on the top of my helmet. The impact drove the helmet down on the bridge of my nose. It didn't hurt the headgear a bit."

Evidence: One of his numerous head injuries. Catching a pass from Bob Griese at the Buffalo 16-yard line, Csonka ran to the 5 where he was tackled and knocked unconscious. "He was pretty badly hurt," says Dr. Herbert Virgin, the Miami team physician. "He had difficulty getting up off the ground. He passed out on the bench. He had a temporary loss of memory." Dr. Virgin wanted Csonka to leave the field on a stretcher and be placed directly into an ambulance for a trip to the hospital. "I walked in here and I'm gonna walk out," muttered Csonka, who then wobbled off the field and eventually got into the ambulance. But he didn't lie down even then. He made the trip to the hospital sitting up.

Evidence: The hardest hit he's ever had. The perpetrator was Roy Winston, a Minnesota linebacker, and he did it as Csonka was catching a pass. "When I started to turn for the ball, I saw Winston coming out of the corner of my eye. I relaxed and I told myself it was time to pay the price. I knew if I tensed up and he hit me going at that speed, my back muscle would split. There was no other way out. When he hit, it felt like an electric shock down my legs. I thought I had injured my spine. But I couldn't just lay there in front of everybody. I had to find out if I was hurt. So I got up and staggered over to the sidelines. Then I thought I'd better lie down and think about it for a while."

Pages upon pages of additional evidence could be presented, but even physicians could become repulsed reading so many medical reports. The point is clear: Csonka has suffered enough injuries to qualify him for a permanent bed at the Mayo Clinic. Yet, the Dolphin fullback hasn't

missed a game since his second season, and in two consecutive years he rushed for more than 1,000 yards.

He is truly a remarkable human being, one who has extraordinary recuperative powers. Take, for example, the Winston tackle. The next time the Dolphins got the ball, Csonka was back in the game.

"I'm not trying to minimize Winston's hit on me," Csonka said. "It was exceptional. I congratulated him when I went back in and he seemed a little surprised. Then he started giggling."

"He really took some pop," Winston commented, "and then he came back. I've been around this game eleven years, and I can't remember getting a better shot at a guy. He is something."

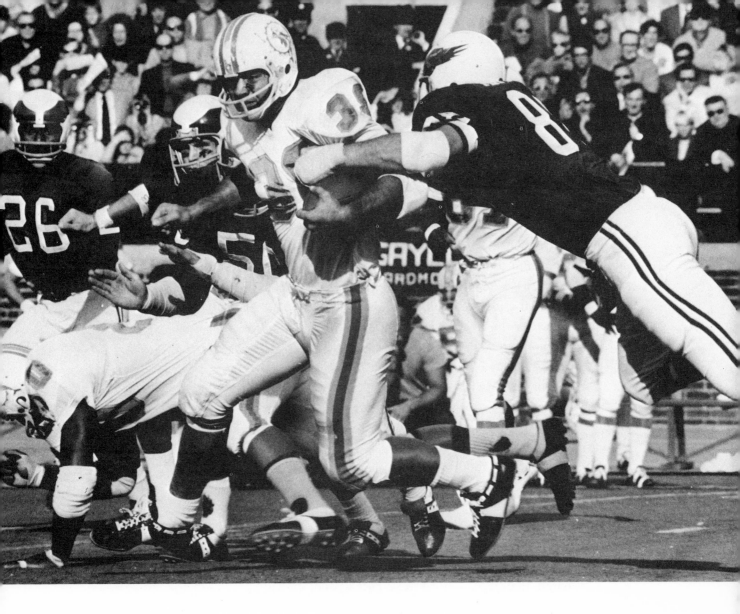

Bob Lundy, the Miami trainer, agreed. "He's a horse," Lundy said. "What more can you say about Csonka?"

There's an awful lot one can say about Csonka. Don Shula, for instance, says, "He is what our offense is all about; he typifies our style."

And Larry Wilson, former St. Louis Cardinal safety, says, "He's like tackling a Caterpillar [the machine, not the insect] with 9.5 speed." But Csonka has his own comments to make about Larry Csonka, and most pertinent to his feelings is the resentment he has for the image that has been created about him.

"The dehumanizing factor is what I don't like," says the 6'3", 235-pound father of two boys. "I resent being called a bulldozer or a battering ram. It reflects a certain type of mentality. When people describe me that way, you think of some creature that erupts from the catacombs with shiny green eyes and a long tail. I'm no primate with his knuckles dragging on the ground.

"When I started playing pro football, I wanted to be a success at it and make a good living at it and it didn't matter to me what people said about me. But as my kids grew older, I realized I had to take my place in society and now I've become pretty careful about what people say. I don't like the idea of people thinking of me as some kind of beast. Hell, I'm just a human being who happens to make a living playing football. I'm no punishment freak. I don't enjoy the pain and soreness that never seem to go away."

Although he didn't know it at the time, Csonka began preparing for the pain and the soreness as a youngster on his family's 18-acre farm in Stow, Ohio. His father, Joseph, is a large Hungarian who always has been a very physical man. "If my father liked you," Csonka says, "he hit you on the arm." And there were many times when he hit people he didn't like.

Larry worked on the farm, hoeing beans, picking corn, baling hay, shoveling manure, digging holes and plowing the fields. He also ran two miles from the farm to the house at supper time each day "because I was so hungry."

"I hated that farm until I was old enough to know better," he says. "I never realized it at the time, but all that work and all that running put me in great shape."

Csonka was in such shape that at the age of fifteen he was 6'1″ and weighed 215 pounds. He was even bigger by the time he accepted a football scholarship to Syracuse University, but he still wasn't satisfied with part of his anatomy. While visiting Syracuse when he was a senior in high school, Csonka encountered a 265-pound tackle named Gary Bugenhagen.

"He had these tremendous forearms," Csonka recalls. "He told me you could make them big by lifting weights, but to really get them tough for hitting, you had to smack them into walls. So he would go around slamming the dormitory walls at Syracuse. Back home that summer before my freshman year, I tried it on our walls."

The only difference was that the dormitory walls were cement and plaster; the Csonka walls were two-by-fours and paneling.

"I tore up a wall in the hall," Larry says. "Then my dad told me to use my own room if I wanted to break something up. I tore up that one, too. So dad called Coach Schwartzwalder and asked him if I could come up early, on my own, paying my own expenses. My dad said the house felt a lot safer with me gone."

The same couldn't be said for Syracuse's opponents once Csonka started playing on the varsity. By the time he had finished leaving would-be tacklers strewn all over college football stadia in the east, he had surpassed all the rushing feats of all the great Syracuse backs—Jimmy Brown, Ernie Davis, Jim Nance and Floyd Little.

When he broke the last record left for him to break, the officials stopped the game and handed him the ball. In the same matter-of-fact way he bounced off tacklers, Csonka tossed the ball to the sidelines. "I didn't know what they were doing," he explains. "I thought the ball was defective or something."

The Dolphins must have thought Csonka was defective when he kept suffering head injuries in his rookie year, 1968. A neurosurgeon suggested he "re-evaluate his occupation" and perhaps find another, and the Dolphins outfitted him with a special helmet that provided his head with extra cushion when it led Csonka's charge into some 260-pound lineman.

Csonka chose neither to look for another job nor to wear the helmet for long. Eventually, the headaches disappeared and the only headache he was involved in was the one he presented to the opposition. It wasn't long before he was making a mockery of the two-word appraisal once put on him by Vince Lombardi. "Too slow," Lombardi had said.

The people whose responsibility he was never thought of him as too slow. Perhaps they were too concerned about the impact of their collisions with him to notice his speed.

There was the time against the Chicago Bears, for example, when Csonka ran for 104 yards and scored on a swing pass from Griese, crashing over cornerback Joe Taylor for the final yards. "I don't want to see Csonka again," the 200-pound Taylor said afterward.

Then there was the time St. Louis safety Roger Wehrli tried to tackle him. "I hit him and bounced back," said Wehrli, who bounced about three feet from where the hit took place. "He runs so low you can't get to his legs. He's got that 'lean' when he runs. He gives you his head and his shoulder but not his legs."

Although such statistics aren't kept, it would be interesting to determine how many yards Csonka gains after he's been hit the first time. The figure would be considerable because when he's hit, he keeps going, dipping low, keeping his balance and driving tacklers back several yards. And once he reaches the defensive backs, there's no telling how many more yards he'll get.

"When a man Larry's size gets past the linebackers and gets rolling, it's all over," says Nick Buoniconti, the Miami linebacker. "The toughest guy I ever saw back there was Cookie Gilchrist in his prime. Nobody wanted any part of Cookie. After a while you'd see those defensive backs start ducking their heads to one side and trying to get out of the way of the shock. Larry inspires that same kind of feeling."

"He seems to seek you out and take you on," says Rich Volk, Baltimore's safety.

But it's not just the "light" defensive backs who respect the tremendous power Csonka has. Fred Miller met Csonka many times in his job as a tackle for the Colts and he came away with this appraisal of the situation: "With him moving with all that power and me standing still, it's a very difficult job trying to stop him. He hits the hole so quickly for his size."

But it's only natural that he takes as much of a beating as he hands out. All running backs do, no matter what their size, because no one can run the ball 10 to 15 or 20 times a game and not feel the interminable pounding by 260-pound people. Csonka feels it, and his injury report shows it.

"I think about getting hurt, but at the same time I try not to think about it seriously," Csonka says. "You can't and still play. But the pain worries me. I sometimes wonder how much longer I'll be able to take it. Pain is a lonely thing. How can you share it with anyone?

"When I play, I get myself into a semi-unconscious state. I'm always conscious of the overall game and what I'm doing and supposed to do, but I try to make myself unconscious of the pain that I know is going to come from carrying the ball. It hurts when people are hitting you and when you run with the ball, you have to be able to accept 'x' amount of pain. I'm not saying this is the worst kind of pain in the world. The pain is there, but it isn't as bad as the pain some poor guy has in a military hospital."

Because of all the hitting they take, running backs have a relatively short life expectancy in pro football.

"It's like walking on top of a glass mountain," Csonka says. "It can shatter that fast. I think Ken Willard [San Francisco back] had the best observation on running backs. He said, 'Playing running back after five years is like playing Russian roulette. You never know when the wrong chamber is coming up'."

In Csonka's case, though, it's possible that the wrong chamber has come up several times but the bullet had more sense than to mess with him.

Mike Garrett

The game, the last of the regular-season schedule of 1970, had just ended and reporters crowded around Mike Garrett in the San Diego locker room. The Chargers had swamped the Kansas City Chiefs, 31–13, and they were helped considerably by Garrett, who only two months before had been a Chief. The reporters, however, weren't simply interested in hearing Garrett's reaction to the two touchdowns he scored. There was another matter they wanted to discuss with him. He had said it before, but they wanted to hear him say it again: this was his pro football finale.

"I wasn't vindictive," the stumpy running back was saying, referring to his performance, in which he also picked up 125 yards rushing and receiving. "I went out there to play football and end a career. This is it. This was my last game. I'm finished with football. I'm sad about leaving because I've met some wonderful people. But this isn't a game; it's a business. Like Dave Meggysey said, it's dehumanizing.

"Anyway, when I signed, I said it would be for five years. But it seems people don't listen. Now comes five years and everyone's surprised. There's nothing to be surprised about. My next career will be a fun career. If it turns out to be the same way, I'll get out of it, too."

What would Garrett's next career be? What was the real reason he was retiring from football, a game he played so well, after only five

years? And why, as would be seen only a couple of months after his fare-well address, did he change his mind and continue playing football?

There are answers to all these questions. First, Garrett was planning to attempt the difficult transition from professional football player to pro-fessional baseball player. Second, he had two reasons—he always had wondered whether he could make it in baseball (he had been as successful at it in college as he had been at football) and he had grown disenchanted with football because of the way he had been treated, especially by Hank Stram, the Kansas City coach. Third, he changed his mind because he got an offer from the Chargers that he couldn't refuse (and that was even before *The Godfather* came out).

Starting at the beginning, or at least at the beginning of Garrett's thinking that led to the baseball-yes, football-no decision, somewhere in Garrett's four-plus-year career with the Chiefs, he became disturbed with Stram and his methods.

"Hank Stram is not my favorite type of person, and he did some things I don't think were very nice," the outspoken Garrett said sometime after his trade to San Diego. "I got to the point where I was being shoveled in and out of games. I just didn't believe in this type of football and I wanted to get out of it very badly. Stram wasn't very satisfied with my running and I wasn't very satisfied with the way I was being used. They had many backs in Kansas City and I knew he didn't need me. I also knew George Allen and the Rams were interested in me. I couldn't see why Stram didn't want to trade me, and all I could see was him thinking, 'I want to keep this guy miserable as long as possible.' I just couldn't see any reason why. I was very upset, and as the situation got worse, as I played less, I was confronted with sitting on the bench. I knew I could play and I didn't like it at all."

Faced with the prospect of never being liberated from Kansas City, which wasn't his favorite town either, certainly not in comparison with his hometown of Los Angeles, Garrett decided he had only one road to take.

"I knew at 27 years of age I still could play in professional sports," said the 5'9", 195-pound Heisman Trophy winner from Southern Cali-fornia. "I was always pretty good at baseball so I felt I would give it a try. I was really sincere about it. Given my situation, continuing in profes-sional football seemed very impossible. I knew that if I made the move the worst thing that could happen was that I could become a failure at baseball. Then I could possibly play football again a little later. But I knew it would get me out of Kansas City, which I wanted to do very badly."

Several years earlier, Mike Garrett the baseball player had been as much in demand as Mike Garrett the football player. It was a situation very similar to that which Brad Van Pelt, the brilliant Michigan State pitcher-linebacker, went through recently. During his junior year at USC, Garrett, an outfielder, was offered $65,000 by the Houston Astros to sign with them, and the next year the Pittsburgh Pirates drafted him and suggested a $100,000 contract.

"I thought he had a chance to be a successful baseball player," says Bob Fontaine, the Pirate scout who recommended Garrett. "He made good contact with the bat and he had excellent running speed. The worst thing about him was his arm, but it was adequate and I thought he had a toughness at the plate which would offset it."

The Los Angeles Dodgers, Garrett's boyhood heroes, were the third team to try and lure him into their outfield, but when the moment of decision came, it went in favor of football because that sport offered a more attractive proposition.

"If I had played baseball," Garrett says, "I would have had to go to the minors and I couldn't be sure I'd ever make it to the majors. In football, I knew I'd find out very quickly whether I'd make it."

The Los Angeles Rams selected Garrett on the second round of the NFL draft while the Chiefs made him a token pick in the twentieth round of the AFL lottery, figuring it was worth just that much of a chance to see if they might interest him in leaving home. To everyone's surprise, even the Chiefs', Garrett signed with them because they offered a financial package that was well beyond anything the overconfident Rams were willing to give him.

But then, four years later, with only one year remaining on that original five-year contract, Garrett said he was willing to play minor league baseball, on the Class A level for the Dodgers' Bakersfield farm club, for only $500 a month. That was a few pennies less than the estimated $9,000 he earned for each month of the football season.

"I'm not out to be a star or make $100,000 in baseball; I'm out to have fun," he said in announcing his intentions to quit football after the

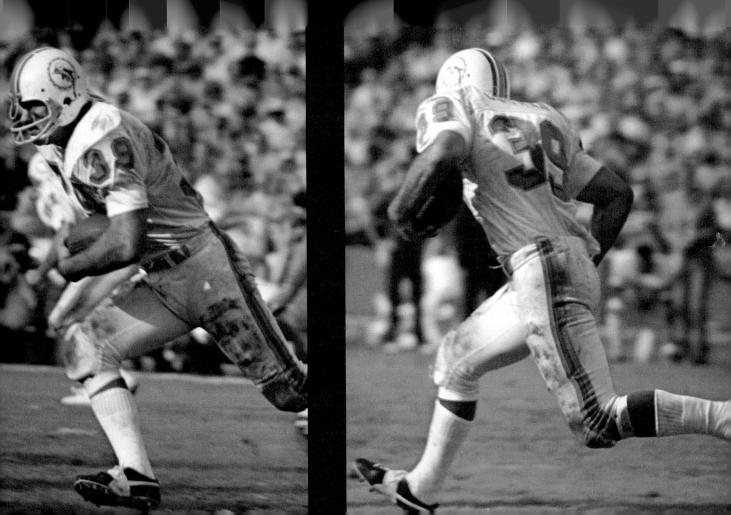

Franco Harris: In command.

Mike Garrett: "Running is music , it's a rhythm, a beat."

Calvin Hill: Coming back, and back, and back . . .

Marv Hubbard: The hard way.

Ron Johnson:
Looking
for the hole.

Franco Harris:
Hit him high and
you lose him.

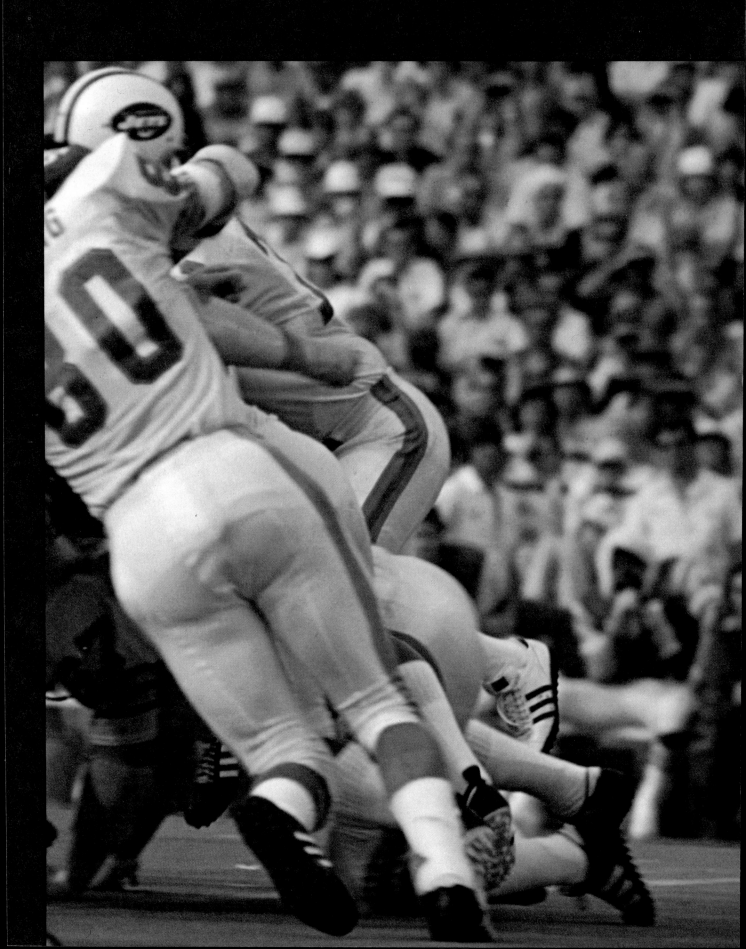

1970 season. "Did you ever want to play the violin like Jascha Heifetz when you were a kid? Well, I always wanted to play for the Dodgers. I was a big Dodger fan even before they moved to Los Angeles and it's always been a childhood dream to play with them. Wouldn't it be nice if I at least tried it?"

Hank Stram, incensed at what he felt was an affront to the Chiefs and to football, didn't think so. He traded Garrett after the fouth game of the season, sending him to San Diego for a second-round draft choice and ending a Kansas City career for Garrett that included two Super Bowl appearances, a rookie year (1966) in which he led the AFL with a rushing average of 5.5 yards per carry and a sophomore season in which he gained 1,087 yards.

The trade, though, didn't alter Garrett's plans. His outlook on football didn't change when his uniform did, because he played sparingly with the Chargers.

"I get traded to a team where they need a running back and I sit on the bench the whole time," he complained. "After the season I called Al Campanis of the Dodgers and told him I was ready to sign."

According to Garrett, the Dodgers were ready to sign him, but his lawyer suggested holding off for a while. The Chargers, meanwhile, told Garrett they'd like him back and shortly before he was preparing to leave for the Dodgers' spring training camp in Vero Beach, Florida, he met with Gene Klein, the San Diego owner.

"The offer," Garrett said, "was attractive enough that we decided it would be ridiculous for me to go into baseball."

"I still lean to baseball, but football is the practical thing for me to do," he explained after signing a Charger contract for a healthy raise. "I decided after much deliberation that my best long-range interests were to continue playing football. I want to emphasize that my desire to undertake a career in baseball was sincere."

The Chargers were pleased; the Dodgers weren't devastated. "It would have been a long shot anyway," said Campanis, a Dodger vice-president. "I'm happy for him. I think he did the best thing."

Garrett, the fourth child of parents who separated when he was nine months old, has done a lot of good things in his life—outside of football as well as in. Raised in a low-rent government housing project located in a black ghetto of East Los Angeles, he spent much of his free time in Kansas City working with disadvantaged kids and continued working in that area when he moved his place of business to San Diego.

His primary avocation has been working with the San Diego district attorney's office as a special assistant involved with establishing a rapport with black and Mexican-American kids. Besides being satisfying to himself and beneficial to others, the job has been an eye-opener for Garrett. "I never thought I would have been called an Uncle Tom, but I have," says the man who more frequently has been called an outspoken, militant black.

Garrett also has been called small—on the football field, that is. The tag was placed on him when he was a rookie in Kansas City and has stuck to this day.

"The first time I ran onto the field for practice with the Chiefs," he recalls, "a fan nearby said, 'They paid all that money for him?' And I was just running out on the field."

Even in the Charger camp, though, they don't let Mike forget that he's not one of the physical giants of the game. "The guys would always kid Jerry LeVias [5-9, 175] and myself about being midgets," he related. "You get tired of hearing this so one day Jerry turned to them and said, 'We play the Chief this week. We two little guys will win the game for you!' They just laughed. Well, Jerry caught a ball to tie the game and I had the touchdown that won it. We just looked at each other and died laughing. If it was a movie, the end would have come right then."

Despite his original intention of playing only five years, the end still hasn't come for Garrett. In fact, the way he played in 1972, his seventh season, he might just be getting started again. Carrying the ball more than he ever did in a season (272 times)—and for that matter, more than any Charger back ever did—he ran for 1,031 yards, the second time in his career he surpassed the magic mark. And he did it in a year in which he wasn't even sure he would have a regular job.

Not too long after training camp began, the Chargers acquired controversial Duane Thomas from Dallas, and it was apparent that all he had to do was show up at camp and he would have Garrett's job. After all, Mike gained a less-than-sizzling 591 yards in 1971. Nevertheless, Garrett wasn't hoping his new teammate would act like the old Duane Thomas.

"Wherever Duane is, tell him to get into camp," Garrett said one day in August while Thomas was AWOL (actually he wasn't absent without leave; he was just plain absent without reporting). "We need him. All we want to do is win and he can help. He's a helluva runner, but he can't help unless he gets here."

Thomas never got there, but just his spirit hovering somewhere nearby seemed to serve as a spark to Garrett, both on the field and inside himself.

"It's a corny phrase, but Thomas made me deal with myself and this has made me a better man," Garrett said one day toward the end of the season. "I probably wouldn't have done so otherwise. If I had been totally confident in myself, I wouldn't have worried. I was full of self-doubt. What was my identity? This is a problem for sensitive, intelligent men—like Duane Thomas."

But the job the Chargers needed done was for someone who was there, someone who was a hard-running, hard-working football player—like Mike Garrett.

"If you'd have told me I had a chance for 1,000 yards, I'd have said you're crazy," Garrett remarked. "This has been such a chaotic but enlightening year."

It certainly beat playing center field on a bunch of Class A baseball fields in the California State League.

Franco Harris

Never before in their long, frustrating history had the Pittsburgh Steelers won a championship of any kind and now, after they had finally won a division title and had come within seventy-three seconds of winning their first playoff game and advancing to the conference championship game, They suddenly found themselves trailing the Oakland Raiders, 7–6.

The Steelers had the ball on their 40-yard line, it was fourth down and 10 yards to go and they had only twenty-two seconds in which to do something to keep their scintillating season alive.

The only thing to do, of course, was to put the ball in the air and hope, and that's precisely what Terry Bradshaw tried to do. The quarterback quickly dropped back to pass but almost just as quickly, the Raider linemen stormed toward him. One Oakland lineman reached Bradshaw and grabbed him, but the 6'4" Steeler squirmed away and darted to his left. After a few steps, though, he encountered a Raider coming from the opposite direction and he started back toward the right.

Suddenly, Bradshaw stopped and threw downfield. John Fuqua, a Steeler running back, was standing near the Oakland 35-yard line, and the ball was heading for him. But Jack Tatum, the safety who had knocked down the previous two passes, quickly raced toward Fuqua and the ball, and when it arrived, it deflected off something (Tatum's shoulder, the officials ruled) and bounced nearly 10 yards backward and toward the ground. At that instant, the Steelers saw their entire season flash before them. As soon as the ball hit the ground, their conference championship dreams would lie shattered there, too.

But incredibly the ball never hit the ground. Seeming to come out of nowhere, running faster than a speeding bullet and leaping many yards at a single bound, Franco Harris scooped up the ball just below knee level and without breaking stride, raced the remaining 42 yards, crossing the goal line with 0:05 blinking on the scoreboard clock and igniting a scene at Three Rivers Stadium that could be rivaled only by a Cecil B. DeMille epic film.

"I saw the ball bounce," Harris explained later, "and I groaned, 'Oh no.' Then I saw it coming toward me. Why was I there? I was just running in that direction figuring I might be able to help in some way."

To say that Harris helped the Steelers in 1972 is like saying the city of Pittsburgh has steel. A rookie who played sparingly in the first four games (he gained only 79 yards), Harris ran for more than 100 yards in seven games (most in the league) and finished with 1,055 yards, just short of the rookie record.

For his efforts, which included leading the Steelers to the best season in their history, Harris was named Rookie of the Year and, perhaps just as important, inspired the creation of Franco's Italian Army.

Now some players have fan clubs whose members dutifully collect

autographed pictures of their heroes and if they're really active, they might hold a meeting or two. That's the type of fan club people are generally familiar with. And then there's Franco's Italian Army.

"The first game of the season we were all sitting in our special Italian section at Three Rivers Stadium and the thought hit me that we needed a hero," says Tony Stagno, a Pittsburgh baker. "My main man, Al Vento, says it would take an army to get these fans going so we made a decision. All of us being Italian and Franco part Italian, why not call it Franco's Italian Army?"

Wearing khaki-colored helmet liners and waving tri-colored Italian flags, the members of the army saluted Harris by eating cheese and drinking wine and cheering him on—with the other Steelers—at all home games and some road contests.

In fact, during the week before a game in San Diego, Stagno flew to the West Coast and in a special ceremony—attended by Harris, who was excused from practice for the occasion—inducted Frank Sinatra into the army. And after Harris's clutch play beat Oakland, composer Henry Mancini wired, "How do I enlist in Franco's Army?"

Interestingly, the United States Army has played a large part in Franco Harris's life. His father, Cad Harris, is black and served with the U.S. Army in Italy during World War II. While there, he met Gina Parenti, an Italian girl whom he married and brought back to New Jersey. They had nine children, of whom Franco (born on March 7, 1950) was the third. The others are Daniella, Mario, Marisa, Alvara, Luana, Piero, Giuseppe and Michele.

As noticeable as Franco is on the field, he is as striking in appearance off it. He is 6'3", weighs 230 pounds, and has an Afro along with a mustache and a distinguished looking semi-beard. His facial features are both black and Italian.

It was this unusual combination of features that led an old man, a stranger on the boardwalk in Atlantic City, to tell him several years ago, "I've never seen anyone like you before. You look like an emperor. You've got a Roman nose, Roman eyebrows, a Roman face. But you're black. Yet you look like an emperor or a mythological god."

That he should have come to the Steelers as some sort of god was not really expected by most people, especially many Steeler fans who through the years had seen their hapless team get burned by one bad first-draft choice after another.

The Steelers, in fact, initially were criticized for selecting Harris rather than his Penn State teammate, Lydell Mitchell, in the opening round. Mitchell had a better record and more publicity as a senior at Penn State, and nearly everyone but the pro scouts believed he was the better player of the two.

Harris, however, had experienced various difficulties in his final year of college. There were injuries, for example, and there was a negative outlook. Harris, it seems, spent much of his final year perhaps believing some of the things he was reading about Mitchell and himself (that Mitchell was the man everyone liked) and he brooded about it.

"I don't think I lived up to my potential," he says. "It was more or less a mental thing. I think I matured mentally with the Steelers."

But Harris's most noticeable difficulty as a football player at Penn State was saved for last: he was demoted to the second team for the Cotton Bowl game against Texas.

"I'd had a hamstring pull and I spent extra time getting taped," Harris explains. "When I reported to the field the team was already into calisthenics. Coach [Joe] Paterno told me if I was late the next day he'd move me down. I tried to get the trainer to hurry up next day, but he took his time and I wound up on the second team."

To Paterno, it was nothing big, simply a matter of discipline. "I'll say this about Franco," Paterno remarks. "He didn't cause any unrest on our team. He took his punishment and when I put him in the game, he went all out. That's the way he is. Sometimes he was slowed by an injury, but I can't remember a game that he didn't make a long run when he was 100 percent healthy."

Paterno wasn't the only one to notice the way Harris played. The scouts did, too, and Steeler Coach Chuck Noll hesitated not at all when his turn came in the first round of the 1972 draft. Harris, on the other hand, wasn't so quick to appreciate Noll's action.

"I was glad to go in the first round," the back says, "but I thought I was going to a loser. People didn't have anything good to say about Pittsburgh, and after the cold winter up at State I wanted to go with a club located in a warmer part of the country."

Once he warmed up though, the climate turned torrid in Pittsburgh.

"I wasn't sure of my ability at first," Harris relates. "Maybe it was a carry-over from previous years. But I decided I had a lot of good qualifications. I decided that it could only hurt me if I played with the wrong frame of mind. Then I wondered how long it would take before my ability came out. I was surprised that I adjusted so soon. In the NFL there's a style you have to learn. Seeing how Larry Brown runs really helped me. When there's a little opening, he flies through the hole and he can run over people and he knows when to put it on. Concentrating on that helped me."

Harris didn't have much experience to learn from in his first four games with the Steelers, but he finally got a chance in the fifth game, against Houston, and he responded by rushing for 115 yards on 19 carries. He suffered a relapse the following week against New England, gaining just 27 yards, but from there on he covered as much ground as a stadium full of artificial turf.

For the next six games he surpassed the 100-yard mark, making him only the second man ever to do that in the NFL. Jim Brown, the yardstick by whom all other runners are measures, is the other. Carrying the ball from 12 to 20 times a game, Harris ripped Buffalo for 131 yards, Cincinnati for 101, Kansas City for 134, Cleveland for 136, Minnesota for 128 and Cleveland for 102.

In trying for his record-tying 100-yard game against the Browns in the twelfth game of the season, Harris nearly didn't make it. With only five minutes to play, he had totaled only 65 yards. The Steelers were winning, 30–0, and ordinarily Noll might have removed Franco from the game. But Noll isn't the steel-hearted (and headed) person some coaches are and he left his first-year gem in so he could match Brown, with whom the coach had played at Cleveland. Getting the necessary yardage wasn't easy; after all, the Browns knew what the Steelers were going to do. Yet Harris ran the ball six times and gained 37 yards and a line in the record book with Brown.

For the season, Harris wound up with the sixth highest rushing total, but his 5.6 yards-per-carry was easily the best average among the ten runners who flooded the 1,000-yard circle.

"What can I say about him? He amazed me every week," Noll says. "He's a more complete player than Jimmy Brown."

After watching Harris plow through his Kansas City Chiefs for 134 yards, Hank Stram said, "He's the most damaging big runner I've seen this year."

Vince Lombardi liked Harris, too, even though the late coach never saw Franco play in person. Sam Huff, the former all-pro linebacker, tells the story of the time the Washington Redskins were preparing for the 1970 draft.

"The assistant coaches were looking at films and we had these films of Penn State," recalls Huff, who was a Lombardi aide at the time. "Franco was only a sophomore at the time but in one of those games he was making some fantastic runs. Lombardi came walking down the hall while we were looking at the film and somebody called him into the room.

"Hey, Coach," the assistant said, "come in here and watch this guy. He's half-black and half-Italian."

"Half-black and half-Italian," Lombardi said. "I'm not interested. He's probably half a runner, too."

Nevertheless, Lombardi went into the room, the coaches rewound the film and the boss watched for about twenty minutes during which time Harris zig-zagged his way to a couple of touchdowns.

"Goddam," Lombardi finally said. "Look at that Italian run."

Two years later, it was Noll's turn to watch Harris on film and drool. Shortly afterward, Harris got his chance at licking his lips when he signed a contract that reportedly gave him a three-year deal for $150,000. But Franco didn't rush out and spend the money. He especially didn't buy a car, which is the first thing many suddenly rich rookies do. Harris, in fact, was so modest about his new wealth that he often rode the bus to Steeler practices in his rookie year.

"I'm not ready to buy a car," he explained. "I like the freedom of riding the buses and hitchhiking on an off day. When I'm ready, I'll get a car. I was thinking of a Porsche or a Mercedes Benz. Then I figured $9,000 or $11,000 for a car is too much."

There are a lot of people in the NFL, particularly the Oakland Raiders, who think Harris is too much.

Calvin Hill

When Calvin Hill was a third grader in the Baltimore suburb of Dundalk, his teacher asked him what he wanted to be when he grew up.

"President of the United States," nine-year-old Calvin replied.

Hill has several more years to go before he can become eligible to fulfill his boyhood ambition, but while he's waiting he isn't doing a bad job of being one of the best all-around backs in the NFL. In fact, his feats with the Dallas Cowboys recall the days when "triple threat" was used to describe a player who could run, pass and kick. In Hill's case, he can run, pass and catch.

There was the game against Pittsburgh in 1972, for instance, when the 6'3", 230-pound Hill ran 23 times for 108 yards and scored 1 touchdown, caught 4 passes for 27 yards and combined with Ron Sellers on a 55-yard touchdown pass.

"What the National Football League needs is a good black quarterback," Hill joked after he passed 36 yards to Sellers, who ran the remaining 19 yards for the touchdown that gave the Cowboys a come-from-behind 17–3 triumph over the stubborn Steelers.

The play started out just like the two Hill turned into touchdown passes as a rookie in 1969. He started out as if he were running a sweep, then suddenly pulled up and whipped the ball downfield.

"The Steeler defenders came up fast and Sellers made a great block fake and went deep," said Hill. "He was so far open I was scared I was going to overthrow him."

But, Sellers said, "It was really a fantastic pass. They were covering me with a linebacker and I just got behind him. Calvin really put it in there."

It was one of the high points of the pro career of Calvin Hill, a career that was still young but that had been dotted with low points. A series of injuries—to toe, back, shoulder and knee—plus the presence (sometimes) of Duane Thomas had hampered Hill's development as a pro running back, but all of those problems disappeared in 1972, and Hill proved just how valuable he could be to the team that had shocked everyone by picking an Ivy Leaguer in the first round of the draft in 1969.

To begin with, Hill ran the ball a team record 245 times and gained a team record 1,036 yards. He didn't break into the upper echelon of the league's passers, but he did lead the Cowboys in pass receiving, catching 43 for 364 yards for another club record for backs. Only one other back, Ron Johnson of the New York Giants, finished among the top ten in both rushing and receiving.

It was obviously an impressive performance by a man who had undergone knee surgery during the winter, after having missed six games the year before. It also was self-gratifying because Hill had begun to

sense a feeling of resentment from his teammates over his perennial physical problems that affected his offensive output.

"It seems you're judged over a long period of time almost more by your ability to stay healthy than by what you do when you're in there," he said before going through his first injury-free season. "I think some of the players resent it and that's frustrating. It's even more frustrating when you think you've done your all, especially when you see guys you don't think are doing the same thing. The reason I've been hurt is that I've been a reckless runner. I've learned you can't really go 100 percent all the time. At least you have to pick your spots. Sometimes you have to go down or run out of bounds."

Explaining what he meant, Hill continued, "Maybe I've just been trying too hard, not giving up or giving in when I should. There were so many times when I was in a hopeless situation with three or four tacklers on me and I'd just keep fighting them. I once hurt my shoulder jumping for two or three extra yards. I hurt my back trying to get Willie Lanier with a roll block when I was out of position. I finally began to realize those are stupid things to do. I know now I should have let Lanier go.

"I used to razz Bobby Hayes for running out of bounds like he does, and he said, 'Well, I always play.' Now I can see his point. Sometimes it might be more important to your team for you to be able to suit up every game than to get a few extra yards."

As football life turned out for Hill, it was more important for his sake to be able to suit up for every game because during the times that he didn't suit up, Duane Thomas did. Then when Hill was healthy and ready to return to the lineup, he found Thomas already in his spot.

"My second year [1970] was the worst," Hill said. "I was out two games and then I was able to play. I'm not saying what should have been done. I think I played pretty well in the first part of the season when the team wasn't going that good. Then I was shoved aside. It was humiliating, a bad experience personally. I know you have to realize what's good for the team, but you also have to think about what's good for you. That certainly wasn't good for me. It was like I wasn't there. At the end of the season I was a nobody."

Hill, who always emphasized that his displeasure was directed at the situation and not the player (Thomas), said he had considered asking to be traded. "I watch Kansas City and wonder what it would be like playing behind that offensive line," he once said. "I wonder what it'd be like if I could play in New York, Los Angeles, Baltimore, Washington or San Francisco."

Hill wasn't made any happier when he was listed as second string behind Thomas entering training camp in 1972. But Hill showed up and Thomas didn't, and the result was that Hill stayed—as No. 1—while Thomas was traded to San Diego.

"I never looked at it as though Duane and I were in competition," Calvin said. "I was hoping someday we might play in the same backfield. We helped each other when we were."

There's no doubt, though, that Thomas's departure helped Hill. There's also no doubt about what Dr. William C. Wade did for him.

Dr. Wade was the physician who brought Hill into the world the day after New Year's Day in 1947 and who was a close friend of the family. When Calvin was ready for high school, Dr. Wade suggested to his parents that he should attend a school outside of the ghetto in which they lived.

"He said I should go to a school where I would face a challenge, both in athletics and academics," Hill relates. "They liked the idea so he suggested they apply to the Schenley Foundation for a scholarship at the Riverdale Country School in New York."

Already growing large physically, Hill blossomed both academically and athletically at the private school and when he was a senior, he chose Yale out of the approximately fifty colleges that sought his services. Although the school wasn't the best training ground for professional football, it certainly did good things for his mind.

"At Yale," he says, "each student must learn to think for himself. I liked that."

What he didn't like, at first, was the course he followed on the football field. He was a quarterback when he went to Yale, but after one practice he was moved to halfback because there was another freshman quarterback, Brian Dowling, who showed great promise.

"I accepted it although I had some small doubts for a while," he says. "I think that any time you have a situation like this, especially when you are black and the other man is white, if you are an aware person you are going to think about it. As it turned out, and looking at it objectively, their objections were valid. If I had been white there would have been no question about it."

Despite his presence at a school where football was just another extracurricular activity, like debating, Hill and his football talents, which grew with each year, were discovered by the Dallas Cowboys. They sent one of their top scouts, Bucko Kilroy, to check him over and test him and he emerged from the routine with results that were as impressive as any college player the Cowboys ever checked. Particularly impressive was his score on the psychological test the Cowboys give. The team doesn't disclose such information, but when asked about Hill's performance on the test, Gil Brandt, Dallas's director of player personnel, said, "Approximately 4,000 athletes have taken our test and Hill scored in the upper two percent."

To the surprise of almost everyone else in the league, the Cowboys made Hill their first draft choice, the first Ivy League running back so chosen since the New York Giants took Tony Minisi of Penn in the first round in 1948.

As sure as the Cowboys were of Hill's talent, though, he wasn't sure what they had in mind for him. When he reported to his first pro training camp, he was tried at linebacker, tight end and running back. "I wasn't sure I could play professional football and I still wasn't sure because of all that moving around," he says. "I learned later they were just experimenting, but I honestly thought at the time they were switching me because they weren't satisfied with my performance at any of the positions. I was certain they were just giving me one last look before cutting me from the squad."

While Hill was shocked at being selected by the Cowboys in the first round, the Cowboy players were more than puzzled. When quarterback Don Meredith heard the news, he asked, "Who's he?"

"A halfback from Yale," he was told. "He's been hurt and he's black and he's a ministerial student."

"That Tom Landry," Meredith said of the Dallas coach. "He don't miss a trick."

It didn't take long for Meredith and the rest of the NFL to find out more about Hill. The rookie rambled for 807 yards in his first nine games and seemed to be a cinch to lead the league and break the rookie rushing record. But then he suffered a freak injury, which was to plague him the rest of the season and set the pattern for his physical problems in the next two years. It was nothing more than a toe injury, but it might as well have been a broken leg.

Suffering a separation in the sesamoid, where the tendon passes over the joint on top of the big toe, Hill played only occasionally the rest of the season. He finished with 942 yards, which neither won the rushing title nor set the rookie record.

The following season, Hill hurt his back and a shoulder and gained 577 yards, and in 1971 he hurt a knee and dipped even further to 468 yards. He was particularly frustrated by the knee injury.

"I thought I was running better than ever at the time," he said, after a tackle by the Giants' Spider Lockhart sent him to the sidelines. "I thought I was reckless, with a certain amount of knowledge. It's ironic and tragic the injury came at the time it did. I was reaching a balance between instinct and knowledge as a runner. I don't know. Maybe it's a sign from God to do something else."

If the injury was such a sign, no one would have known it better than Hill. After all, while he was playing for the Cowboys, he also was attending Southern Methodist University's Perkins School of Theology. He eventually gave up theology as a possible future career, but he didn't give up football as his present occupation.

Instead, he was determined to come back completely healthy (he did) and win back his job in 1972 (he did), then play all fourteen games and help contribute to a Super Bowl appearance (the Cowboys didn't)

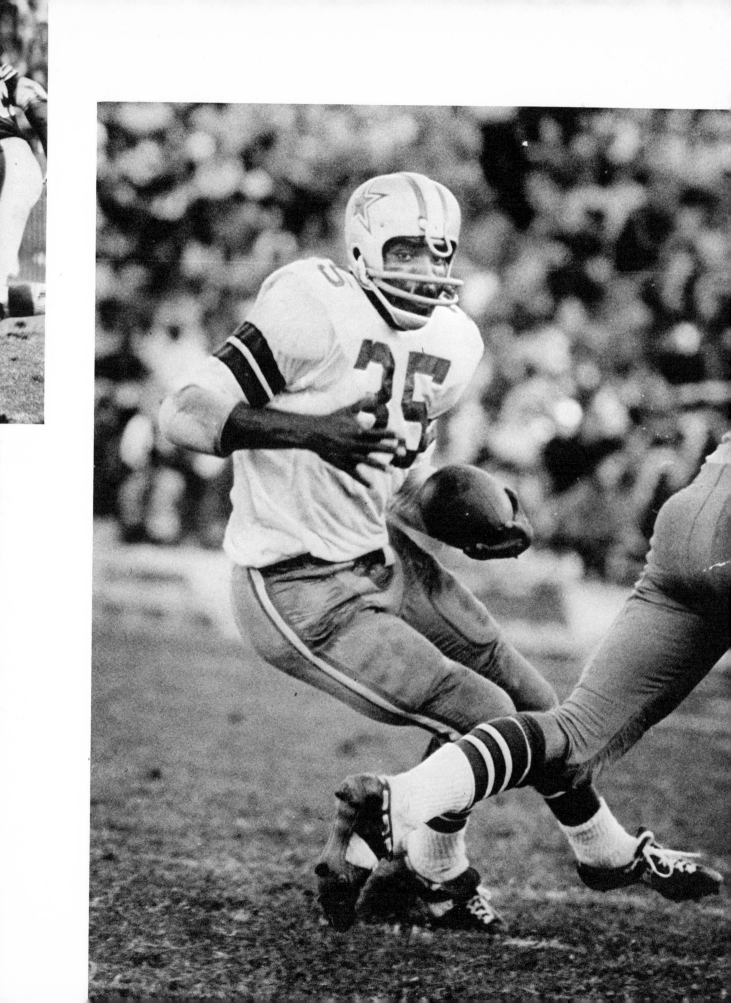

in which, unlike the first two Dallas was in, he could participate meaningfully.

"My desire," he said before the season began, "is to realize my potential over a whole season. If that means gaining 500 yards—which I hope it doesn't—then all right. I could look back and say I had done it. I don't think anyone ever does [fulfill his potential]. But the closer you come, the happier you are. I haven't really felt that way yet."

Hill worked diligently toward gaining that feeling. The first indication of his attitude was his performance in the Cowboys' incredible Functional Weight Test, which is enough to drive any but the most super of human beings into a less demanding pursuit, such as putting labels on cans.

The FWT, which the Dallas players swear was originated by the same fellow who made a pact with Joe Hardy in *Damn Yankees,* is a collection of 26 (few people have survived to count them) "exercises" that must be completed in no more than 26 minutes. It is the ultimate test of strength and endurance and it is pure torture. No one ever had completed it in less than 17 minutes. Coming back from knee surgery, Hill finished in 16 minutes, 44 seconds. After that, gaining 1,000 yards and leading the Cowboys in pass receiving was easy.

Marv Hubbard

Marv Hubbard, says George Blanda, "is like an old fire horse raring to go. His eyes flash fire and I swear there's smoke coming out of his ears."

When he first reported to the Raiders, though, Hubbard more closely resembled a foal than a fire horse, and his eyes were filled not with fire but with awestruck stares. As for his ears, they weren't large enough to take in all the listening and learning Hubbard had to do to reach a point of competitiveness with the rest of the rookie crop.

"I had thought about playing pro ball, but I really didn't know what I wanted to do," says Hubbard, who was drafted by the Oakland Raiders in the eleventh round in 1968. "When I joined the Raiders' camp I was in absolute awe of players like Daryle Lamonica, guys I had seen on television, and I didn't have any confidence in myself. I was lost. I didn't know anything about formations. I think we used about two of them at Colgate. I wasn't a very good blocker because I never did much blocking in college. And I couldn't tell you a thing about defense. Guys who go to Big Ten schools or a place like Southern Cal know more about football after their freshman year than I did when I got out. I was really a green kid."

Because he realized how green he was, Hubbard didn't turn red with anger when the Raiders cut him. He simply went on his way, after rejecting a Raider suggestion that he play minor league football in San Jose for $250 a week. His next stop was Denver, where he tried for a job with the Broncos, but he soon departed that camp, too, after he became involved in a conflict with another player. The Broncos also suggested he could play minor league football for $250 a week, but Hubbard refused that, too, and instead headed home, which was located in the tiny village of Red House, New York.

"I had been away from my family [his wife, Ginny, and a daughter, Allyson, then 2] for a long time," he recalls. "My morale was low and I was frustrated. I also was afraid that if I didn't make the minor league team, I'd really be finished."

Back in Red House, which can be found, if you look fast enough, about sixty miles south of Buffalo, Hubbard pondered his future. He had a degree in economics, but he wasn't sure where that could take him.

"Then one night, I was sitting at the kitchen table talking with my dad and he was saying that $250 a week isn't that bad," Hubbard says. "Just then the phone rang and it was the general manager of the Hartford [Connecticut] Knights. They were in the Atlantic Coast League.

"At that time I didn't want to play and was ready to say no, but he told me they could get me a job with a construction company in Hartford. That was something I had been thinking about wanting to do so I said, okay, I'd give it a try."

Before he could make that try, though, Hubbard had to recover from the shock that struck him when he reported to Hartford. "That had to be one of the lowest moments of my life," he says. "Their locker room was about as big as the Raiders' training room and we didn't have lockers, just nails to hang our clothes on. We kept our equipment in a canvas bag."

From that low point, Hubbard zoomed straight up, leading the league in rushing, with 899 yards in only nine games, and catapulting himself back into the sights of pro teams. Several were interested in signing him to a contract for the 1969 season, one for $15,000 more than the Raiders had signed him for the year before. But before he could take advantage of the sudden interest in him, he received a telephone call from Al Davis, the man who runs the Raiders as if they were a combination of the CIA and the NKVD.

"You can't sign with anyone else," Davis told him, "because you're already signed with us."

Davis went on to remind Hubbard that he had signed not a two-year contract with the Raiders in 1968 but two one-year contracts, a perfectly legal transaction. In other words, when the Raiders released him in 1968, that terminated the first contract, but the second remained in effect for 1969.

"I wasn't resentful about returning to Oakland," Hubbard says, "but I was skeptical because they'd already seen me once."

The Raiders, however, had seen Hubbard as a 215-pound candidate for a tight end job. At least that's what Davis had in mind for the youngster. When he returned, Hubbard weighed 230 pounds and he was a running back with promise (a promise, as things turned out, to knock down anyone who got in his way).

It's difficult to say someone has made a comeback if that person never has been anywhere in the first place, but Hubbard indeed made a fine comeback from his failure to make the team in 1968. In fact, he overcame not only that negative beginning but also a 230-pound roadblock that had been placed in his way. The roadblock was a fullback named Hewritt Dixon, one of the most bruising runners in Raider history.

Hubbard originally gained Dixon's spot in 1971, when he was injured, but even after the veteran was healthy again, Hubbard held on to the spot and climaxed his delayed start to the top by rushing for 1,100 yards in 1972, a team record and fifth best mark in the league that season.

The determination Hubbard displayed in making that long and

difficult climb was reminiscent of his experience in college after he flunked out in his junior year.

"At Colgate," he explains, "I was more of a hot dog than a hot student. When I flunked out, that shook me up. I returned and hit the books hard for the first time. I made up my credits and did B-minus work my senior year."

When he finally won a job with Oakland in 1969, it was as if he had to make up his pro credits in a hurry. He could run with the ball and knock down people who got in his way, but he still had much to learn about other phases of the game. This point registered very clearly in a game during his rookie year.

"George Blanda was the quarterback, and on one play I ran out for a pass and the linebacker didn't cover me," Hubbard relates. "So I came back to the huddle and told George. He called the same play and looked over at me. I knew it was coming. I got so excited I just took off

and watched the linebacker go right by me. He was blitzing and I was supposed to pick him up. Hell, I just waved as I went by and he really got to George. George didn't like it and I never forgot it either."

There are many defensive players in the NFL who haven't forgotten Hubbard—after they've tried to tackle him. Hubbard doesn't look like someone who would mug a fellow football player in the middle of a football field, in front of 60,000 people and in broad daylight. He has a kind face, almost cherubic, but then, he doesn't hit tacklers with his face. Just with every other part of his body.

"I want to hit tacklers as hard as I can," he says, "because intimidation is what this game is all about. I've got to intimidate them, get them worrying about me hitting them. I can't let them intimidate me."

Hubbard, of course, doesn't succeed in intimidating everyone he hits, but that doesn't create a lack of respect in anyone he encounters.

"Nobody comes at you harder than Marv Hubbard," says Willie Lanier, Kansas City's bear-like linebacker. "He gets mad when you tackle him and I guess that's the way it should be. We keep pounding him and he keeps right on coming. I've never seen anyone quite as determined as Hubbard."

The toughness that Hubbard displays run after run had its birth back in his teen-age days in Red House. "You had to be tough, else the town boys would just keep beating up on you," he says. "But the fights weren't really serious. You might slug it out with a guy and later have a drink with him. I remember one time my best friend and I got into an argument while we were driving home. We stopped the car, walked out on the field and had it out. It seemed to be the best way to settle things."

In growing up and maturing, Hubbard harnessed his excess energy and now puts it to profitable use. It frequently shows up in Oakland games.

There was the time in his rookie season, for example, when the Raiders were playing Kansas City, their arch rivals for the Western Division title. The Raiders were leading, 10–6, and all they had to do to ensure winning the division title was hold on to the ball for the final 5½ minutes of the game. Even though Hubbard was a rookie, they gave him the ball six times and passed to him one other time as he gained 50 of the 70 yards Oakland gained before the gun signaled the end of the contest.

He was rewarded with the game ball, the first he ever received. "It's the biggest tribute any player can receive," he said at the time. "It means more to me than being selected to an all-star team."

Two years later, Hubbard was selected to an all-star team, getting a spot on the American Conference squad for the Pro Bowl when Baltimore's Norm Bulaich withdrew because of an injury. It took the Connecticut state police to find Hubbard to tell him he had been named to the team (he and his wife were vacationing) and the National Conference probably wished they had had a police riot squad to quell Hubbard once he got into the game. He played only the second half, but he still led all runners in yardage gained.

For several seasons now, Hubbard also has led all backs on the Kansas City Chiefs' most wanted list. He rose to that prominent spot following the second game between the teams in 1970. Hubbard was so keyed up during the game that he kept shouting at the Kansas City linemen, "Look out, Big Red, we're coming at you. Here I come." His zealous enthusiasm then carried over to a televised post-game interview, during which he said such things as, "I'm at my best against these guys; I love to beat them more than anything else"; and "We ran the Chiefs into the ground"; and "The Chiefs are a bunch of cheap shot artists."

The volume of Hubbard's fan mail picked up considerably in the few days after that appearance; most of the letters were from the Kansas City area, offering suggestions for what he could do.

The animosity continued to grow, reaching a feverish peak in 1972, when Hubbard was quoted as saying, "We're going to kick some tail when we get to Kansas City." He later denied making that remark, but the denial never caught up with the statement, and the Chiefs' fans reacted boisterously to the Raider runner whenever his name was mentioned over the public address system.

"That didn't bother me," Hubbard said. "What did get to me was that two grown men spit right in my face when I was coming off the field."

Nevertheless, Hubbard enjoys playing the Chiefs perhaps more than any other team. "I think it's easier to play a team like Kansas City that you know is physical," he says. "If we think we're playing a team we can finesse, I don't think we play as well. I know the Chiefs are going to come after us and I want to be ready. There's no danger of us ever not being ready or playing too cute against the Chiefs."

But as fired up as Hubbard gets for the Chiefs and anyone else and as much growling as he does when he gets on the field, there's another side to him that isn't seen by the football public. It was pointed out in an especially vivid way in September, 1972, after a Raider rookie, Ray Jamieson, was in a head-on collision with a punt returned and was removed from the field almost completely paralyzed.

Hubbard went to the hospital after the game and stayed until three o'clock the following afternoon.

"I know how lonely it can become for a rookie," Hubbard explained. "I realized that Ray had never been in Los Angeles. He had no friends, and the doctors and nurses were strange to him. I thought I could be of some comfort. So I stayed."

Hubbard's opponents never evoke that kind of compassion from him.

Ron Johnson

In pro football, a player doesn't get to make too many decisions for himself. His team is decided for him in the draft, his employment status is decided by the coach and, if he's a running back or a receiver, the number of times he gets the ball is determined by the quarterback. Perhaps that's why it was so surprising that Ron Johnson was able to make a decision himself.

The decision involved Johnson's knee and he made it contrary to the wishes of his team, the New York Giants. Johnson injured the knee in the ninth game of a season that already had been fouled up by another injury and an operation. Now a decision had to be made about the timing of operation No. 2.

"They [the Giants] wanted me to wait to have the operation, but the doctor was sure I would need it eventually so I wanted it done as early as possible," Johnson explains. "The team's feeling was that with five games to go, if I stayed off it for two weeks, maybe I could play the last three games. But that frightened me more than the operation—waiting two weeks and coming back and running on the knee and maybe damaging it more.

"A lot of guys were saying, 'Don't get the operation,' but there comes a point when you have to make a decision for yourself. It was my decision, my career, and I'd have to live with it. I imagine I could have come back if I had had the operation after the season, but I just wanted to make sure everything would be all right. I figured there wasn't too much I could have done in 1971 so I wanted to make sure everything was all right for 1972."

Fortunately for the Giants, they didn't argue with Johnson's decision. The torn cartilage in his left knee was repaired, he sat out the rest of the 1971 season and he was all right for 1972. Was he ever all right for 1972!

After playing in just five quarters in 1971, his second season with the Giants and third in the league, the Detroit native ran for 1,182 yards, third best in the league; scored 14 touchdowns, best in the league; and caught 45 passes for 451 yards. His total yardage of 1,633 yards was second only to Larry Brown's 1,689 and exceeded the 1,514 yards he led the league with in 1970.

"I worked as hard as I could to make sure the leg would be ready," says the man who was primarily responsible for making the Giants go in 1972. "I worked out six times a week and I played some very, very tough basketball. I was convinced before I got to training camp that I had it all back. I wasn't worried about being hit because I had taken a lot of bone-to-bone hits on the knee playing basketball and I knew it was all right."

The knee was all right and Johnson was much more than just all right, but as particular a player as he is, he wasn't entirely satisfied with the season that fifty other running backs gladly would have accepted for themselves.

"I think more about the times when I didn't do something right," he said on the eve of the final game of the year. "I expect the highest possible performance out of myself. I feel I should have a good game every week. I'm more concerned about what I don't do."

The Cleveland Browns were concerned about what he wasn't doing in 1969, his rookie season, and that's why Johnson became a Giant. The trade was one of the best the Giants ever made and one of the worst the Browns ever made, and it so delighted Johnson that late in the 1970 season he asked a friend to express his thanks to Art Modell, the Cleveland boss, for "exiling" him to New York.

"He did me the biggest favor of my life," Johnson explained. "You hear a lot about New York and what it means to play for a professional sports team in that town. But you can't really understand it until you get there. The trade was the biggest break I'll ever get in pro football and I'm serious about thanking Modell for sending me over here."

The question, of course, arises: Why did the Browns want to get rid of someone who in each of his first two healthy years after leaving Cleveland rushed for more than 1,000 yards? The answer appears to lie on two levels—problems Modell had with Johnson before he started playing and problems Johnson had on the field after he started playing.

To begin with, the All-American halfback from the University of Michigan wanted much more money than Modell was willing to give him. That in itself isn't unusual in any player-owner situation, but their differences of opinion were compounded by another matter, one that had nothing to do with football. Modell wanted Johnson to join a National Guard unit that several Browns belonged to, but Johnson said he preferred to make his own arrangements.

"That comes under the heading of private life and the Browns were not going to get into my private life," the player says. "That didn't make him overjoyed with me. I guess he got the idea that I was a trouble-maker, but I wasn't. All I wanted was enough money to make me feel I was being paid what I was worth and the right to keep my personal affairs personal."

On the field, everything started out fine as Johnson subbed for an injured Leroy Kelly in the season opener and ran for 118 yards and scored 2 touchdowns. But once Kelly recovered, two games later, there seemed to be little need for Johnson's talents. He either sat on the bench or played fullback, which meant blocking for Kelly or carrying the ball in those infrequent moments when Kelly needed a breather.

"With the Browns," he says, "they only use two backs because the rules say you've got to. They just want to give the ball to Leroy. I began to feel like I wasn't there."

As the weeks went by, Johnson began to lose his confidence and

his concentration and he wound up on the bench. "The coaches told me I was developing bad habits," he says. "I wasn't improving. I was holding the ball in the wrong hand and I wasn't getting off the mark fast enough. I think they were right. I was doing those things wrong."

By the end of the season, Johnson had gained 471 yards, but he was a disappointment to the Browns' brain trust. That's why he wound up going to New York in the second part of a peculiar Cleveland double play. It was peculiar because the Browns were the ones who were out on both ends of the play.

First, in order to get a choice spot in the first round of the 1970 draft so they could select quarterback Mike Phipps, the Browns gave Paul Warfield, perhaps the game's best wide receiver, to Miami. Then, finding it necessary to replace Warfield, they sought Homer Jones from the Giants. And they got him—for defensive tackle Jim Kanicki, linebacker Wayne Meylan and Johnson.

Three years later, another Cleveland team, the Indians, were to trade away another Johnson although this Johnson's best years seemed to be behind him rather than ahead. This Johnson was Alex, the outfielding brother of Ron, and people in sports who know them both always are intrigued that they actually are brothers. Ron is an amiable fellow who gets along with everyone; Alex is a sullen person who keeps to himself, preferring much of the time not to talk to anyone, including teammates.

"Actually, I'm much closer to Alex in personality than people realize," says Ron, the youngest of five children of a Detroit trucking contractor. "The only difference is that I'm the eternal optimist. Alex is the kind of person who, if he doesn't like something, you're going to hear about it. It doesn't matter who you are. If I'm really any different, it's just that I've learned from his mistakes. I've learned to be a little more diplomatic."

Alex is five years older than Ron, but they frequently played together when they were growing up. Both managed to avoid the pitfalls that are rampant in ghetto life.

"We didn't live good, but we weren't rat-poor," Ron says. "My father was home and he had a regular job and we were very close as a family. I think that that more than anything else kept me straight. Sure, lots of guys I knew went bad or got into trouble, but that was them. I knew what I wanted."

Ron wanted to go to college and that he did, receiving a degree in finance from Michigan, where he also happened to play some football. He didn't play much football as a sophomore and before his junior year started he almost was turned into a defensive back to fill a hole. He was kept at halfback, however, and started both that season and the next. The highlight of his collegiate career came in a game against Wisconsin in his final year, when he gained a record 347 yards. Not to be overlooked, though, was the 2,440 yards he gained rushing, which eclipsed the school record established by the legendary Tom Harmon.

Two years later, Johnson shattered another record, this one Eddie Price's Giant high of 971 yards rushing. Johnson rambled for 1,027 yards, and curiously, it marked the first time a runner playing for a professional New York team reached the 1,000-yard perch.

The Giants naturally were ecstatic and eagerly looked forward to the 1971 season, with the feeling they could ride the quarterbacking of Fran Tarkenton and Johnson's running to at least a division title. But instead of climbing into a Rolls Royce for that, they wound up in an old Hudson.

When Johnson reported to training camp, they learned that he had suffered a deep thigh bruise in a pickup basketball game in Detroit. The Giants tried to eliminate the problem with heat treatments and medication for several weeks, but when the ailment persisted, it was decided an operation would be necessary to remove a blood clot that had prevented the muscle from expanding normally.

It was to be a minor operation, and Johnson, the Giants said, would be ready to play by the season opener. Which season opener, though, they didn't say. They meant the one in 1971, but that came around long before Johnson did. The 6'1", 205-pound back finally had recuperated sufficiently to play against Minnesota in the seventh game of the season, and he battered through the rugged Viking defense for 89 yards.

The following week he plowed through San Diego's defense for 67 yards in the first half, but in the third quarter he reached backward for a pass and when he turned back he was sharply slammed to the ground. Once again, the injury was mistaken for a minor problem, a minor leg injury, the Giants called it. But two weeks later, X-rays revealed torn cartilage in the left knee, and that's when Johnson decided immediate surgery was the only solution.

"It was by far the most frustrating time of my life," says Johnson, who never before had suffered a serious injury. "I felt useless. I couldn't contribute anything. All I could do was sit on the bench in street clothes and hope we'd win. At times I felt alienated from the team. The feeling of being powerless was just awful. It's an experience I hope I never have again."

It's a statement the Giants echoed loudly because without their No. 1 runner, the team totaled 1,461 yards rushing, which was just 434 yards more than Johnson gained by himself in 1970.

Johnson's experience in 1972 was entirely different from that of 1971. He worked hard to regain all of his strength, playing basketball (without being hurt) and exercising religiously. When training camp opened with a two-mile run in 90-degree heat, Johnson didn't fool around. He raced along the course and sprinted the final 200 yards, clearly showing he had no lingering problems with his legs.

If any doubts remained, Johnson completely dispelled them in the third game of the regular season when he resembled the prototype of the workhorse. He ran the ball 36 times for 124 yards and caught 5 passes for 60 additional yards. As if that weren't enough, he scored all four Giant touchdowns in the 27–12 victory over Philadelphia, three on passes and one on a run. The 4 TDs were a club record, and league statisticians discovered later that his 41 offensive plays were a league record for non-quarterbacks.

There's one mark, though, that has gone unrecorded. That's Johnson's nonstop daily chess games with teammate Bob Tucker. And when Tucker checkmates Johnson, which he does on occasion, it's a feat that isn't matched too often on the field by Giant opponents.

Floyd Little

Floyd Little, the widely heralded All-American halfback from Syracuse, had experienced a miserable rookie season with the Denver Broncos and now, in his second year, he wasn't doing much better. He had averaged less than three yards a carry as a rookie and his sophomore average was only slightly better. The Broncos were having their troubles as a team, too, and the victories were coming at a considerably more infrequent rate than every Sunday.

But they were leading the Buffalo Bills, 31–29, on this particular November day in 1968, and the victory looked secure because they had the ball and less than a minute remained. Suddenly, though, the gloom that had engulfed them so often set in. Little, running a sweep to eat up vital seconds, fumbled the ball, safety George Saimes recovered and raced 27 yards to the Denver 10-yard line. A field goal later, the Bills led, 32–31, with just twenty-nine seconds to play.

"I felt nothing," Little recalls. "I can't really describe it. All I knew was one thing—I had to run 100 yards some way or other, or I had to quit. I wouldn't have had any other choice. Here were forty guys who worked their tails off in a football game for sixty minutes and one guy had turned around and blew it all. In one play it was gone."

Determined to eradicate the depression and betrayal he felt at the moment, Little literally begged quarterback Marlin Briscoe to throw him a pass after the kickoff. "You've got to let me make it up," he told Briscoe.

The quarterback responded to the halfback's plea and called the play, a pass on which the quarterback heaves the ball and hopes the receiver is in the area to fight for it. Little raced down the field and Briscoe fired.

"When he threw it," Little says, "I knew I was going to catch it. I had to catch it. That's all there was to it. I didn't care who was there. I was going to get it."

And he did, his bowlegs propelling him high into the air and his strong hands picking the ball out of the hazy sky at the Bills' 9-yard line. It was a 59-yard gain and it set up a field goal that brought the Broncos the victory, 34–32.

It would be dramatic to be able to say the Broncos went on from there to win the championship, but the Broncos don't win championships; they're grateful for every victory they gain. But for Little, it was a turning point from which he went on and started displaying the talent that enabled him to surpass the collegiate achievements of fellow Syracuse alumni Jim Brown and Ernie Davis.

"After that day," Little explains, "I developed a new attitude. I didn't let brooding over a past mistake force me into making a new one as I used to. One of the things you learn as a pro is that the other guys are good, too, and they're gonna beat you on some plays. You've just got to forget it and fight back on the next play. You've got to take the long view of the season. You have to psyche yourself to do your best no matter what."

From a low rushing gain of 381 yards in 1967, Little steadily increased his production to 584 yards in 1968, 729 the following season, 901 in 1970 and, finally, a resounding 1,133 in 1971, which was more than any other NFL back gained that year. Winning the rushing title over such bigger backs as John Brockington and Larry Csonka was particularly pleasing to the New Haven, Connecticut, native because all his football life he had to fight the stigma of size.

"When I came up to the pros, everybody said I was too small," relates Little, a 5'10", 195-pounder. "They still say it. Every time I go on the field I've got to prove myself again. The same thing happened back in school. People said I'd never get to college. Then they said I'd never graduate. I've always been prejudged. I've had to fight for everything I got."

Little especially had to fight to overcome the disappointment he suffered as a rookie, when he averaged just 10 carries a game and 2.9 yards a carry. There were various reasons for the meager output, including a lack of experience overall on the young team and a reluctance to give Little the ball more than a relatively few times a game.

"You can't learn anything by carrying the ball once in a series," Little explains. "You've got to carry three or four times in a row. That's the only way you know what your guards are doing and what the defenses are we're running against. When you carry the ball four or five times in a row, you can say, 'Well, this guy's playing it this way, if I duck in, he's been coming in, I can go outside of him.' You have to set a guy up and whoosh."

Little went "whoosh" as a runner and he went that way, too, as he became the recognized leader on the Broncos, the man to whom a younger player could turn for advice and who could make suggestions when he thought a player wasn't doing the right thing.

There was the time, for example, when Lou Saban, then the

Denver coach, was harsh on Bill Thompson, a rookie, after he had fumbled a punt return. Little approached Thompson afterward and said, "He's not attacking you, Bill, he's attacking the mistake and what it means to the team. Relax, learn from it and forget it. It happens to all of us. Just don't brood on it."

At other times, Little uses deeds instead of words to show leadership. In a game against the New York Jets, the Broncos had held the ball for just six plays in the first quarter and were trailing by 13 points. As Little and Thompson dropped back in a punt situation, Little turned to Thompson and said, "We need a big play. They've got to have a lift."

As the punt spiraled into Denver territory, Little stepped in front of Thompson, took the ball at the Bronco 47 and scooted to the New York one-yard line before he was tackled. He scored on the next play, and the Broncos went on to win, 21–19.

"I've never seen a look of such pure determination on a man's face before," a Denver player said of Little on the punt return. "You just knew he was going all the way and you knew things were going to be all right."

Things always weren't all right for Little in the past. As the youngest of six children, he struggled with the rest of his family after his father died of cancer when Floyd was six. Even before he reached junior high school, Floyd hustled to make money any way he could. He sold newspapers, he worked as a stock boy and he shined shoes.

He wasn't quite as good at doing his school work as he was at finding ways to earn a few extra dollars, and when he finished high school his grades weren't good enough to get him into college. But he went to prep school for a year and then caught the attention of about fifty colleges.

In an attempt to recruit Little for Syracuse, Coach Ben Schwartzwalder brought along a "salesman," a former Syracuse player by the name of Ernie Davis. Floyd was impressed.

"It wasn't just his being an athlete," Little says. "It was his whole character. He had this casual way of speaking. He was so unaffected. He'd come and visit me and there was no big entrance like you'd expect from an All-American. He'd just walk in and say, 'How ya doin'?'"

Davis died of leukemia not too long after one of these visits. When Little heard the tragic news, he says, "I sat down and got sick. Right then I knew I was going to Syracuse."

Davis never was very far out of Little's mind, and the thought of Ernie and leukemia was especially present during Little's last season at Syracuse.

In the fourth game of that season, against Navy, Floyd injured his ankle. He should have rested it for a week or two, but instead he continued to play. "I didn't care about myself," he says. "I thought my presence in the lineup would inspire the guys."

The injury, however, was so painful that he began worrying about the ankle. He lost his appetite and he lost weight, dropping from 197 pounds to 182. He also had term papers to do, and all the worries piled up. Meanwhile, he was living on vitamins, wheat germ pills, doughnuts and cookies, "a lot of junk," as he put it.

Little's fiancée wanted him to have a checkup at the infirmary, and the coach told him he had done enough for the team and he didn't have to play the rest of the season. But, although he kept thinking he had some sort of disease, he refused both suggestions. "I thought maybe I had leukemia and, of course, I thought about Ernie," he says.

It wasn't until the university chancellor called him in and told him to get a checkup that he finally consented. "I had to take blood tests four, five times, and that really worried me," he recalls. "They didn't tell me anything except they told me to come back again and again. I didn't know why they kept having me back, and they wouldn't tell me. This really shook me up."

Finally, the doctors told Little what his problem was. He had an iron deficiency, a problem that was cleared up in a few days by iron pills. A similar problem was to plague him in each of his first two seasons with Denver and to serve as a contributing factor in his early problems.

One of his problems has not been his bowlegs, which are more bowed than any legs this side of Roy Rogers. Little's legs turned into parentheses because when he was a baby, he tried too early to emulate his older brothers and sisters who were walking. "I started walking at eight months, and my body was too heavy for my legs," he explains.

As a child, he tried to straighten them by tying belts around them at night, but it didn't work. Now he sees his oddly shaped legs as an asset.

"If I have a good stride going and I'm hit from the side, it doesn't knock me down," he says. "My knees won't hit each other because they'll never meet. And if some guy comes in and gives me a pop on the side of the leg, my knee just straightens up into a normal position instead of getting all banged up. Straighten me up and I'm a good 6-2."

Neither his size nor his legs makes Little timid when it comes to hitting a much larger defensive player with a block. That was one aspect of his game he had to learn when he became a pro, but as with the rest of his game he has learned it well. And in no way does he shy away from hitting. Floyd enjoys telling about the time he and Jim Nance, his 240-pound teammate at Syracuse, were matched against each other in a practice game.

"I used to kid him I'd knock him into the bleachers if I ever got a chance," Little relates. "In this game I broke loose with only him between me and the goal line. I could've faked him easily, but instead I drove right into him. Oh my. We both went ten yards straight up. It was beautiful."

Once Little started driving through opposing defenses, it was a beautiful sight for the Broncos, as beautiful as the poetry that Little learned to love in college. He had wanted to be an English major, but he chose history instead because he felt his grammar left much to be desired. Nevertheless, he got into poetry and even sprinkled a little of it into his banquet speeches. Diners at a sports banquet somehow don't expect to hear lines from Browning, Tennyson and Wordsworth, but he gave it to them. "You ought to be there when I give them Thoreau," he once said. "That's real strong stuff."

Little came out with some pretty strong stuff of his own in 1971, the day Lou Saban announced he was leaving the Denver coaching job. Little had grown to have tremendous respect for Saban and when he was asked for his reaction to the coach's departure, he said, "He just did something I've been thinking of doing. I think it's the type of people playing the game now. Every year they've got a little different attitude. They don't understand what the game is and what it means. One game I had to almost bodily kill a couple of guys at half time for their attitude. They just don't have the attitude like the Costas and the Durankos and the Currents. You can't get them to do anything extra. I don't mind. I want to do it. It's part of the game. But the game itself doesn't mean as much to them. I saw a couple of guys out there last Sunday who could have done more. It's things like this that make you want to say the hell with it."

Little, however, didn't say to hell with it. Instead, he kept plowing on, his own attitude unaffected, and wound up reaching the 1,000-yard plateau for the first time and leading the league.

"When the announcer at San Diego said I'd reached 1,000 yards," he said, "I got goose bumps all over."

A goose-bumped, bowlegged man in knickers might be a funny sight to the casual observer, but there's nothing funny or casual about Little.

Mercury Morris

As the Miami Dolphins assemble on the Sugar Bowl field for a team picture on a day prior to the 1972 Super Bowl, a lone figure sits halfway up in the stands. Technically he isn't a spectator, but emotionally he is.

"I'm just sitting here to get away from what's going on down there; I don't feel a part of it," says Eugene (Mercury) Morris, the Dolphins' kick returner and second-string running back. "I've regressed as far as my participation is concerned. The ironic thing is that the better I've done, the less I've played. I don't know. I'm not the head coach. He got us here and I guess I should be happy. I can't complain. We're in the Super Bowl. But, well, you just want to be a part of it."

The time moves six days ahead, to Sunday, and the scene shifts to the Dolphins' locker room. Super Bowl VI has just been played, and the Dallas Cowboys have wiped out Miami, 24–3. Mercury Morris left the bench only to return four kickoffs and to go to the locker room at half time and following the game.

"I think the longest time I was on the field was for the national anthem," Morris tells the newsmen who were unfortunate enough to draw the losers assignment. "It's sad, man. A lot of times I just wanted to run out there myself. Just put myself in the game. I'm like this. I'm beyond thinking I can do it. I know I can do it. Any time an offense like ours can only put three points on the board, regardless of who we're playing, something has got to be wrong. Not that they were that great. It's just that we didn't come out and play like we were supposed to. I'm sour grapes, man, about a lot of things.

"We stunk and we lost. I felt there was something I could do. I felt like I could run on those damn guys. I know of no reason why I didn't play more. Man, it hurts so much when I have to sit my ass on the sidelines and watch this stuff going on, knowing there's something I can do. I expected to play today because he [Coach Don Shula] said he was going to try to get outside on them. We tried it and it didn't work and then we started to beg for situations, as opposed to us dictating the situations that we want to be in. Now everyone's walking around here sad."

The time and scene again change, this time to a year later and to a field in Long Beach, California. Once again it's pre-Super Bowl picture day and this time Mercury Morris is right in the middle of everything, eager to smile at the birdy and say cheese.

"The only argument Shula and I have now," Morris says, "is that he thinks he wants us to win more than I do."

With both Shula and Morris and all the other Dolphins working diligently and feverishly, Miami beats Washington, 14–7, in Super Bowl VII and no Dolphins are sad. They are ecstatic, none more so than Morris.

What has happened in the intervening year to so drastically alter Morris's outlook on Super Bowl life?

Well, for one thing, a conversation. "Coach Shula called me to his hotel room the next day and we had a meaningful discussion," Mercury says. Out of the discussion came an understanding, an understanding that Morris would get a chance to play more as a running back in 1972 than he did in 1971.

And out of the understanding emerged one of the best performances by a running back in the NFL. It was a performance that helped the Dolphins win all seventeen of their games and it was a performance that was enough to change even Scrooge's disposition.

Replacing Jim Kiick as the feared second half of the Dolphin's potent running attack (the first half is Larry Csonka), Morris scored a league-leading 12-touchdown rushing, raced for precisely 1,000 yards and finished with a 5.2-yard average, the same as Csonka and one of the best in the league. In his first three years in the NFL, the Pittsburgh native had gained a total of 834 yards. His presence on the field did not go unnoticed.

"The improvement of the Dolphins this year," George Allen, the Washington coach, said before the Super Bowl, "can be attributed to one thing—No. 22. He's been the difference."

"It's not so often you see a guy who has so much speed and moves like that," adds Buddy Ryan, defensive line coach of the New York Jets. "Trying to tackle him is like trying to catch an escaping balloon."

His own teammates noticed him, too. Comments Norm Evans, an original Dolphin and a fine offensive tackle: "If guys like Buoniconti, Griese and Csonka are the heart of this team, Merc's the soul."

In his first three seasons with the Dolphins, after they selected him in the third round of the 1969 draft, Morris was a threat each time he entered the game to turn a sweep into a long touchdown run. But no matter how well he did—he averaged six yards a carry—his potential was blunted somewhat by the defensive knowledge that whenever he came in, he very likely would run with the ball.

"When he came in, it was for one play," says Bobby Bell, the excellent Kansas City linebacker. "That was his play. All you did was key on him."

But once Shula started using him more, the threat he represented became even more dangerous.

"Morris adds a lot of threat on the outside," Bell explains. "He's got good moves, he's quick and he's a good runner. You find a lot of backs with speed who don't know how to follow blocks, but he does."

You also seldom find players who'll be as outspoken as Morris, but then how many have majored in speech therapy in college?

College for Morris was West Texas State, which was more than a football's throw from Pittsburgh's Avonworth High School, where he was one of only two black students and where he scored 34 career touchdowns, none from less than 21 yards out.

At West Texas State, Morris acquired the name Mercury, which he doesn't particularly like (it was given to him by an Amarillo sports writer); drew seventeen write-in votes for mayor of Amarillo; and set a major college career rushing record of 3,388 yards, many of them with the aid of his blocking back, Duane Thomas.

Miami didn't need a mayor; nor, for that matter, did the Dolphins

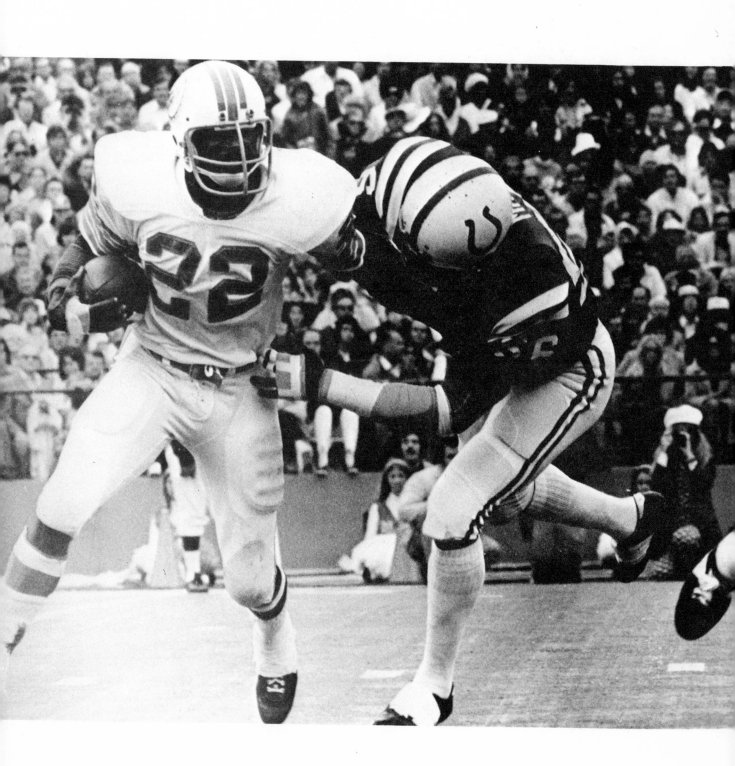

need another starting running back. They already had Csonka and Kiick, and that was Morris' problem.

With both running positions more than adequately filled, Morris was used almost exclusively as a kick returner in his rookie year and did well, leading the American League in kickoff returns after scampering 105 yards for a touchdown against Cincinnati. The following two years he was used less as a kick returner and not much more as a running back. What really upset him, though, was Shula's use of him in 1971, when he ran the ball fewer times than he did in 1970.

That was the prelude to his pre- and post-Super Bowl anger and frustration, and his outburst, in turn, served as a basis for endless off-season rumors that he would be traded. Morris, however, wanted to remain in Miami, and Shula wanted to keep him there.

"I didn't expect to be traded; I wasn't hoping to be traded," the muscular Mercury says. "People didn't realize the intensity of the situation. You don't get a chance to win the Super Bowl but once a year, if then. I felt I could have added to our offense, but I didn't play. If you analyze the things I said, all they meant was, 'Why didn't I play?'"

Shula understood what Morris meant; the coach just didn't like the platform he used for stating it.

"I can understand an athlete being disappointed because he wants to play," Shula says. "It shouldn't be any other way. But if he has a complaint, he should come to me first."

In their meeting the day after the loss to the Cowboys, the two reached an understanding that the following season would be different.

"The opportunity at training camp was all I really wanted," Morris explains. "In 1971 some people were saying, 'Well, if Jim gets hurt, you'll play more,' but I didn't want that situation. That's not a healthy situation for Jim or for me."

The ideal situation, as far as Shula was concerned, was a three-back plan in which he would use all three—Csonka, Kiick and Morris—inter-changeably. He had wanted to try it for the previous two seasons, but each time something happened in training camp to prevent it. In 1970, Morris suffered a severely hemorrhaged thigh in the first summer practice, and that knocked him out for a while. Then in 1971 Kiick and Csonka held out early and Morris later sprained an ankle.

In the team's six exhibition games prior to the 1972 season, Morris proved Shula's idea could work, at least from his standpoint, because he ran for 346 yards on 50 carries, one of which went for 79 yards.

"You have to call them all first stringers," said Shula, who considered himself fortunate to be burdened with such a problem.

For his part, Morris was pleased, too. "You have some things you have to prove to yourself," he said. "For me, it was proving I could start for this club."

And so it was that when the season started, if Butch Cassidy and the Sundance Kid weren't broken up completely, they were nudged apart a little by Black Bart. Csonka ran the ball 213 times, Morris 190 and Kiick 137 in the regular-season schedule. In post-season play, Csonka had 51 carries, Morris 41 and Kiick 34.

Whereas Kiick gained only 521 yards during the season, though, Morris and Csonka became the first two players ever to reach the 1,000-yard plateau with the same club in the same year.

To achieve that historical feat, Morris needed 95 yards entering the final game against Baltimore. Even though the Colts were keying on him because they knew the Dolphins would be giving him the ball frequently, the 5'10", 190-pound flash crept closer and closer to the magic mark as the game neared the end.

But then, twice in the closing minutes, Morris limped off the field with a twisted ankle, and after the second time Shula refused to risk further injury by letting him return to the game to try and get the 9 yards he still needed.

A few days later, though, Mercury picked up the necessary yardage. At the request of Mike Rathet, the Miami public relations director, league officials viewed the film of the Dolphins' game with Buffalo in October and discovered that a scoring error had charged Morris with a 9-yard loss on a fumble that he never had touched. The 9 yards were restored to his record and that gave him 1,000.

"The commissioner made the decision," a league spokesman said, "and everyone who saw the film had to agree."

Everyone who saw Morris play last season also had to agree that he had improved in the areas of his play that perhaps had induced Shula to use him infrequently in the previous two seasons. He was a better blocker and he held onto the ball more securely than in the past.

Of all his achievements, though, one that Morris enjoyed as much as any other was the game he had against the Bills on November 6. Running on the natural grass that he prefers to artificial turf, the 25-year-old Morris broke three tackles on his first carry of the game for a 33-yard run that set up a field goal, and on the Dolphins' next possession, he broke three more tackles and dashed 22 yards for a touchdown.

In all, he ran for 106 yards on 11 carries (a 9.6 avearge), caught one pass for 26 yards and returned a kickoff for 30 yards. O. J. Simpson, meanwhile, ran for a mere 45 yards in 13 carries. The one-sidedness of their performances delighted Morris.

"It's much more satisfying when I do it against O. J.'s team," he said at the time. "Back when I was in college, O. J. beat me out two years in a row for the collegiate rushing title. Simpson always seems to beat me out. When we play Buffalo, we always play the team. But for my own personal vendetta, I go against O. J."

Thus, it appears that whether Morris seeks revenge or parity on the field, he gets it.

O.J. Simpson

It was the day of the 1973 National Football League draft, and the ballroom of the Hotel Americana was filled with tables, telephones and club employees sitting at the tables and manning the telephones. On a terrace to one side of the ballroom, spectators, the first of whom had gathered before eight o'clock that morning for the non-show, were busy keeping track of the players selected, arguing over the wisdom of those choices and predicting which players would go next.

Six teams already had made their first-round selections and now it was the Buffalo Bills' turn. Suddenly, as if were a fall Sunday afternoon at Shea Stadium and the Jets were driving for a touchdown, the fans started yelling.

"Get O. J. some blockers," one teen-ager shouted.

"Give him a line to run behind," someone else implored.

And minutes later, when it was announced that the Bills had selected "Paul Seymour, tackle, Michigan," many in the crowd erupted into a burst of applause and cheers.

The scene vividly related two facts about O. J. Simpson: he is popular among football fans, whether or not they're Buffalo enthusiasts, and everyone knows how dearly he could use a decent offensive line to help him unleash the talent that flows from him.

Simpson's talent is such that in 1972, running behind a line that more closely resembled a field hospital in Vietnam, O. J. Simpson gained 1,251 yards and led the league. Furthermore, he recorded the season's longest run in the league, 94 yards aganist Pittsburgh, and he produced the best one-game performance in the American Conference, 189 yards against the Steelers. That total was 2 yards shy of Larry Brown's league-leading total amassed against the New York Giants, but in that game Brown ran the ball seven more times than Simpson did in his big game.

Nevertheless, most "experts" considered Brown the No. 1 running back in the league. True, they said, Simpson gained 35 more yards than Brown, but Brown missed the last two games of the regular season. What they didn't add in Simpson's behalf was that the Washington line was both healthier and better than Buffalo's.

Of the six players who had been expected to fill the Bills' five interior line positions, two were lost early with knee injuries, one developed a kidney problem on the first day of training camp and another missed the last five games with pinched nerves and bone spurs. In addition, the replacement for one of the players lost before the season began with a knee injury also suffered a knee injury and missed the entire season, too. Nevertheless, there was O. J. slashing and cutting and fighting his way toward the kind of yardage everyone expected him to accumulate when he entered pro football as the Heisman Trophy winner and the "best college player" of the sixties.

Simpson, who couldn't produce more than 742 yards in any of his first three excruciatingly frustrating pro years, was so ecstatic about the year he had in 1972 that he could hardly wait to get started on 1973.

"I don't usually begin to prepare for the season until May," Orenthal James Simpson said one day in February, "but I've been lifting weights. I don't like to lift, but I'm doing it. Everybody is getting ready for this next season."

Simpson's attitude showed a remarkable change in him from his previous seasons with the Bills. When he played for Southern California, he was playing in a location he enjoyed, he was playing for a winning team, he liked the coach and he was running the ball an average of 32 times a game. With the Bills, however, he was playing in a place he didn't like, he was playing for a loser, he didn't like the coach and he was running an average of 14 times a game.

Nothing much short of a trade or the recruiting of the reincarnation of Vince Lombardi's Green Bay Packers could have altered Simpson's place of business or the success of the company he worked for. But he certainly believed a change of coach or a change in the coach's thinking could have changed his mental outlook. The culprit, in his eyes, was John Rauch, the man who coached the Bills in Simpson's first two years, 1969 and 1970.

"The way Rauch used me just took all the fun out of the game," he said. "I wasn't happy because I wasn't carrying the ball. I felt my career was leaving me. You get down because you look around the league and see runners that aren't as good as you or no better, but they're doing so much better in the statistics. Some were carrying the ball 50 to 100 times a season more than I was. I was used to carrying 20, 30 times a game. After a lot of games in my first two years I wasn't even puffing. It's frustrating to feel so fresh after a game. At USC I was used to being beat-up after a game. With Buffalo I finished games as fresh as when I started. When you feel that fresh, you don't feel you've played a game or done anything for your team."

After leaving the Bills, Rauch suggested that Simpson was naive and laboring under some false impressions when he became a pro.

"With as fine a defense as USC had," he coach said, "they could afford to wait for O. J. to break the game open for them. But with Buffalo, we'd get down by 14 points early in the game and we'd have to start playing catch-up. You can't play catch-up by giving the same guy the ball on every play and waiting for him to break one."

Simpson, of course, didn't feel any better about the Bills' having a bad enough team to fall behind by 14 points early in a game. If they had been able to go ahead by that much with him carrying the ball only a relatively few times a game, the situation might have been more tolerable. But that wasn't the case either.

At the same time, O. J. wasn't the only back ever to go through such a dilemma. Not everyone can play for a Super Bowl champion, and it's obvious that the better a collegiate player a fellow is the higher he'll go in the draft and the lousier the team he'll play for.

Once, at the end of a game between Buffalo and Denver, Floyd Little, the Bronco back who preceded Simpson into the league by two years, walked over to O. J. on the field and said, "My first two years at Denver were terrible. We had the same guys in the offensive line as we do now. It takes time to build a line. But we have an adequate one now. Hang in there. Your day will come."

In a wild coincidence, Simpson's day came under the same coach

who hastened Little's day—Lou Saban. The coach of the Bills' 1965 AFL championship team, Saban returned to Buffalo in 1972, after one year at the University of Maryland and five at Denver, where he helped turn Little into a rushing champion. Based on Saban's reputation and his first days in training camp, Simpson was impressed.

"Coach Saban came to us with a winning attitude," O. J. said. "He has changed the attitude of a lot of people."

He especially changed Simpson's attitude and his status on the team. Whereas he never had run more than 183 times in a season, Simpson carried the ball a team record 292 times and it paid off in the rushing title. It also paid off in more thrills for Simpson in one season than he had had in the first three put together.

There was, for example, the Bills' 27–20 upset of the San Francisco 49ers, the team Simpson fanatically followed as a youngster growing up in a San Francisco ghetto.

"This has to be the greatest thrill in pro football," he said after piercing the 49er defense for 138 yards on 29 carries. "Just think, when I was a kid, I idolized the 49ers. I didn't even miss a game from 1957 to 1965. When I was a kid, Al Cowlings [a Buffalo teammate] and I used to sit up in the end zone stands at Kezar Stadium. After the games, we'd try to go out on the field just to take a close look at John Brodie and Charlie Krueger. And to think we not only got a chance to play against them, but we beat them, too. What a thrill."

Later in the season Simpson thrilled himself and the Buffalo fans by romping 94 yards for a touchdown against Pittsburgh. It was the kind of run football fans had come to expect of him when he was at USC but one they hadn't seen him display as a pro.

"Dennis Shaw called a play that I really didn't think would work," he related. "I was supposed to stutter-step to the left while our guard pulled. But I was afraid he'd get there too quick so I hardly stuttered at all before I followed him. As I got there, Reg McKenzie hooked the linebacker inside. Then J. D. Hill chopped down the corner back. Suddenly I was one-on-one with the safety with a chance to wiggle on him, stiff-arm him, whatever I needed. Once I get out there, it's my game. I just took off."

Simpson kept taking off all season until, finally, after three years of frustration in the eleventh game of the season he reached the 1,000-yard mark. It happened on the last play of the Bills' 27–10 loss to the Cleveland Browns. Simpson wasn't happy that the team lost, but he was flattered that his teammates had decided in the final minute to help him get the yardage he needed to attain the goal of every running back.

Three games later, with Larry Brown sitting on the bench and watching, O. J. ran for 101 yards, leading the Bills to a surprising 24–17 triumph over Washington and capturing the league rushing crown.

"I didn't run any differently than before," he said afterward of his finest season. "I just had better blockers and a coach with a system geared to running."

Commented the coach: "I don't think he's even scratched the surface of his talent yet."

Saban referred to football, but his statement may hold true for other aspects of O. J.'s interests as well. For instance, the amiable O. J. has exhibited a blossoming talent for acting and has acquired a fine sense of finance, in which he has become involved as an outgrowth of his football prowess.

Probably no other player in professional sports history ever has started out with such lucrative off-field interests as Simpson did. Even before he had touched the ball as a pro, O. J. had hooked up with Chevrolet at a reported $250,000 for three years, Royal Crown Cola at a reported $120,000 for three years and the American Broadcasting Company at a reported $6,000 per sports event for two years. Combined with his four-year, $215,000 salary plus a $100,000 loan from the Bills, that package wasn't bad for a fellow who with his wife and baby had lived on $125 a month at USC and who before that, while growing up, lived with his family in a government housing project or an attic in a house of a friend.

Nor was it a bad beginning for a fellow who almost had his football career cut off before it started by coming within a lie of being thrown off the high school junior varsity football team.

On the day of a big game, Simpson and two teammates were spending some time shooting dice in a bathroom at school. They all crapped out, though, when Jack McBride, their coach, walked in and found them playing their little game. Many coaches in that situation would simply warn the players never to do that again and let them go. But McBride, in a move for which Simpson later could be thankful (even though he escaped punishment), took the boys to the dean's office.

"When we went to the dean's office," Simpson recalled, "the other two guys, Joe Bell and Al Cowlings, walked in front of me. Coach McBride told the dean he caught us shooting dice in the rest room. He gave the dean the dice and left. When he did, the dean told me to close the door. So I started out and began to close the door from the outside, but the dean called, 'Where are you going, O. J.?' So I said, 'I wasn't shooting craps. Coach just asked me to help him bring these guys down.' Then the dean told me I could go and the other guys got suspended."

The other two boys, one of whom (Cowlings) later became

Simpson's teammate at USC and Buffalo, couldn't resent O. J.'s little ploy. "They thought it was pretty smart for me to think that quick," Simpson said. "Al said there was nothing he could say about it. He said if I could get away with that, I deserved it."

More than ten years later, Simpson's teammates don't resent anything he does or gets either. With the talent he has and as valuable as he is to the team, they feel he deserves everything he gets—especially the ball.

Linebackers

Nick Buoniconti

When he was two years old, Nick Buoniconti almost drowned. When he was three, he fell out of a moving car. At six he was hit by a truck, at eight he had scarlet fever, at nine he broke his arm and at twenty-eight he almost retired.

Of all those calamities, the last undoubtedly would have been the worst if Buoniconti had followed through on his original intention.

"At first I very seriously thought of quitting football and becoming a lawyer fulltime," says Buoniconti about the trade that sent him from the Boston Patriots to the Miami Dolphins in 1969, seven days after he passed the Massachusetts bar examination. "I wasn't particularly excited about going to Miami and living there after I had worked to set up everything in Boston. The Miami heat bothered me, too. I recalled how awful playing one game a year down there had been, and I seriously wondered if I could take the practice sessions, a half dozen exhibitions and seven regular-season games."

However, Buoniconti finally decided he would join the Dolphins if they gave him a three-year contract. "It was the security I needed to move my family and my life," he says. At first the Dolphins were reluctant to agree to the deal, but then they relented, too, and from there built one of the league's stingiest defenses around the league's smallest middle linebacker.

If Buoniconti had retired, the Dolphins probably would have eventually found another middle linebacker who could do an adequate job. There aren't too many around, though, who do the job as adequately as Buoniconti.

If he had retired, Buoniconti would have become an attorney but eventually would have been just another name (albeit a long one) in the massive list of lawyers in Boston's Yellow Pages. In choosing to continue playing, however, Buoniconti has become an attorney in Miami's Yellow Pages; president of All-Pro Graphics, Inc., a player licensing firm; a restaurateur; a celebrity; and an indispensable member of two Super Bowl teams, one of them the most successful team in pro football history.

All this from a player whose college coach wouldn't even recommend him to any NFL team and all this from being tossed away in one of the most dubious trades in recent football history.

The Nick Buonicontis of the football world aren't too often given away like an unused rake in a garage sale, especially after they have been named to the all-AFL team six of the seven years they have played, and are not surpassed in popularity among their team's dwindling number of fans.

But Clive Rush, the Patriots' new coach, wasn't going to let that kind of reasoning interfere with his plans. He wanted to get rid of Nick and he had eyes for a lineback, John Bramlett, and a reserve quarterback, Kim Hammond.

"I never got the complete story of why I was traded," the Springfield, Massachusetts, native says, "but from what I picked up afterward it came down to three things. When Clive Rush learned what my salary was [around $40,000], he said he wouldn't pay any linebacker that much [Rush was an offense-oriented coach who had worked with Joe Namath in New York]. Second, I had a bad knee and they thought I couldn't come back, and three, there were assistant coaches who were accusing me of being a clubhouse lawyer."

So Buoniconti took his salary (which was to get even higher in Miami), his knee and his diploma from Suffolk Law School and headed south. There he felt at home because in 1969 the Dolphins were losers just like the Patriots. Nevertheless, Buoniconti soon grew very fond of Coach George Wilson, and when he was fired after that season, Nick felt "like my father had died. He had given me great responsibility."

He felt even worse as he tried to master the defensive strategies of Don Shula, the new coach who used a highly disciplined defense compared with the free-lance style Buoniconti had played in Boston.

"We blitzed about half the time in Boston," he explains. "I was more or less on my own. I was always trying to play my position and a part of another position. In Shula's defense, you have a primary responsibility and you take care of that. If you can do that with time left over to do something else, then you can help out. But the first thing you do is protect your territory."

For the first half of the 1970 season, this was easier written on the blackboard than done on the field for Buoniconti. "I was really discouraged," says the Dolphin who, on his tallest and heaviest day, is 5'11" and 220 pounds. "I'd had a pretty good career in the AFL and now it looked like I couldn't do anything right. I guess it was after our seventh or eighth game that year that I came into the dressing room really down. Don asked me to come into his room and told me he knew how I felt. 'It takes maybe eight or ten games to learn this defense,' he told me. 'You're doing a real good job. Just quit worrying. You're going to make it.'"

As with most things, Shula knew what he was talking about because Buoniconti did make it. And the fact that he did was a primary reason the Dolphins zoomed from a 3-10-1 record in Wilson's last year to 34-7-1 the next three, with an added 5-2 record in the playoffs.

"Nick's two great qualities are quickness and intelligence," Shula says. "He's really not tall enough to play middle linebacker, but his anticipation is so good that he's always in the right place. And he's quick as a cat."

The cat particularly growled in the playoffs leading up to the Dolphins' first Super Bowl appearance following the 1971 season. In the

first game, the longest ever, against Kansas City, Buoniconti blocked a Jan Stenerud field-goal attempt in the first overtime period, leaving Miami alive until Garo Yepremian could win it with a field goal of his own in the second overtime period.

Then came the conference championship game with the Baltimore Colts, who, behind the masterful direction of John Unitas, had wiped out the Dolphins with a ball control game a few weeks earlier. This time, though, Miami shut out the Colts, and the losers gave a large share of the credit to the Miami man in the middle.

"To run the ball on Miami effectively," said Unitas, "you have to be able to block Buoniconti. Today we couldn't do it. I thought he played an excellent game and was the key to their defense."

Buoniconti was particularly instrumental in halting a Colt thrust that could have changed the tone of the game. Baltimore had the ball at the Miami 9-yard line and needed 2 yards on fourth down for a first down. Miami was leading, 7–0, and the safe move would have been a field goal, but Coach Don McCafferty wanted to get to half time with a 7–7 tie, so he ordered a try for the first down.

The play Unitas called was designed to get Don Nottingham up the middle for the necessary yardage behind center Bill Curry, who was to block Buoniconti. But the Dolphins cut off Curry by sending a tackle over the middle, and Buoniconti stopped Nottingham at the line. The Dolphins took over, and Baltimore never got that close again.

Buoniconti's play in the playoffs so impressed the Dallas Cowboys, the National Conference champions, that they seemed to talk about and plan for Nick the entire week prior to the Super Bowl.

"In a way, it's easier to cope with Butkus than Buoniconti," said Dave Manders, the Cowboys' center. "Butkus knows you're coming at him and will wait for you. His idea is to overpower you anyway and then get on with his business. Buoniconti is so quick he just eliminates you and starts right toward the action. He doesn't worry about what's going on around him. He reacts that fast. We'll have to stop him from doing that."

The Cowboys' obsession with neutralizing the most important ingredient in Miami's defense paid off. Running a lot of counter plays, where the flow of the play goes one way and then the runner slants back in the opposite direction, the Cowboys were able to keep Buoniconti away from the ball frequently enough that they won with ease. They were further aided by the knock on the head that kept Nick in a fog for a good part of the game.

Whether he was disturbed at having the blame for the loss placed on his bulky shoulders or he felt he was being flattered too much by the suggestion that he was that vital to the Miami defense, Buoniconti ridiculed the idea that the Cowboys won because of him. He used the Dolphins' Super Bowl victory the following season as evidence that he was right.

"When we lost to Dallas, all I heard was how it was my fault because they influenced me on the cutback plays," he said. "Washington tried the same thing, but our defensive line made the difference and the Redskins couldn't contain them."

No one could contain the Dolphins' defense in 1972. The unit, tagged the No-Name defense because it was said to have a bunch of names no one heard of, allowed just 171 points during the regular season, an average of 12 a game. And spearheading the unit was Buoniconti with 72 tackles and 74 assists, both high marks on the team.

Despite his obvious importance to the defense, Buoniconti rejected any suggestions that he was its star. "We don't have any superstars playing defense," he said. "We're just a bunch of hell-raisers and street-fighters and good-time guys."

Buoniconti was a good-time guy during his senior year at Notre Dame in 1962 after he signed with the Patriots for the hefty sum of $10,000 in salary and $1,000 in bonus. As soon as he signed, Buoniconti spent the bonus money on a two-day-long party for his friends. "One thousand dollars was a tremendous amount of money for us in those days and we threw it away," says his wife, Terry.

Buoniconti undoubtedly would have received a much larger bonus had his college coach, Joe Kuharich, not wiped out any chance he had of being drafted by an NFL team. "I'm sorry, Nick," Kuharich told him before the draft that was an integral part of the war between the two leagues. "You certainly played good football for us. But I don't think you're big enuogh to play pro football and because I don't, I won't recommend you. It wouldn't be right."

Thus, it was left for the Patriots to take him on the thirteenth round of the AFL draft and sign him for much less money that a free agent commands today when there is no war.

"I knew I better sign for what they offered," Nick says, "when I threatened to go to Canada and they offered to pay my way."

In one sense, it was perhaps fortunate for Buoniconti that he went with the Patriots because it doesn't seem very likely that a player of his size would have received a shot at middle linebacker with any of the established NFL clubs. He probably would have become a lawyer sooner and today he would still be in Boston, sitting in some law library studying precedents instead of game plans.

That, of course, would be fine as far as people like O. J. Simpson are concerned. "He gives me the biggest problems of any linebacker," Simpson says. "He knows where you're going before you get there."

Buoniconti wasn't always that bright. Otherwise, he might be wearing a uniform number in the 50s or 60s, more typical of a linebacker than his distinctive No. 85. The explanation for that number goes back to his rookie season.

"My number was 66, but on all our kicking teams I was an end," he relates. "Well, if you're playing a pass receiver's position and you don't have a pass receiver's number, you have to report to the referee when you go in the game. In our first game Gino Cappelletti was getting ready to try a field goal for us, and as I went in our coach told me, 'Don't forget to report.' So I forgot. Gino kicks the field goal and the next thing I see a flag down—15 yards for not reporting. The coach said, 'Why didn't you report?' And I said, 'I just forgot.'"

Stunned by such brilliant reasoning, the coach didn't say anything else. Instead he instructed the equipment manager to give him No. 85.

"Hey, I got the wrong number; I had 66 last game," Nick told the equipment man when he saw the new uniform.

"Coach says you get 85 from now on," came the explanation. "Now you don't have to remember to report—just remember to block."

Buoniconti hasn't forgotten much since then, including how happy he has to be for changing his mind about retiring between Boston and Miami.

Dick Butkus

It's not enough that Dick Butkus is brutal, violent, rough, fierce, awesome, nasty, intimidating and just plain virtually impossible to keep away from the ball and the man who's trying to hide it from him. Now he goes and gets tricky, too. Not as a middle linebacker, a position he plays as if he invented it. No, the way he plays middle linebacker he doesn't have to be tricky.

But, you see, Dick Butkus has another job. He blocks on Chicago's kicking teams, and that's where he gets tricky—not throwing blocks but calling fakes. Butkus received the new assignment from Coach Abe Gibron in 1972 and, like a kid with a new toy, he had an absolute ball with it in one particular game, a contest in which the Bears upset the Minnesota Vikings, 13–10.

Butkus intercepted a Fran Tarkenton pass in the game and ran the ball into winning field goal range, but that routine play would have had little significance without the fakes. There were two of them—a fake field goal and a fake punt.

The way the strategic command is set up, if Butkus feels he'd like to call a fake kick, he notifies Gibron by a hand signal. Then, if Gibron approves, he nods his head, which is large enough so that Butkus has little trouble seeing it.

In the first instance against the Vikings, the Bears lined up for an attempted field goal by Mac Percival. But Bobby Douglass, the holder, took the ball and ran 6 yards for a key first down.

Later, Butkus tried the old hand-signal-head-nod trick again, and this time Bobby Joe Green, the punter, passed 23 yards to Cecil Turner for another important first down.

Perhaps Gibron got the idea from a game the previous season when the Bears edged the Redskins, 16–15, on an impromptu extra-point pass from Douglass to Butkus. That play was really tricky because not even the Bears expected it.

Cyril Pinder set up the play by reaching 40 yards for the tying touchdown early in the fourth quarter. Percival came on the field to kick what could be the winning extra points, and Butkus lined up in his blocking back spot. The next thing Butkus knew, though, was the snap was high and Douglass was scrambling around trying to find someone to throw the ball to.

"When I double-teamed on the end," Butkus explained, "I turned around to see how close they got to the kick. Then I heard the crowd roar and saw Bobby scrambling, so I took off for the end zone and started waving."

Douglass saw two Bears, Butkus and Willie Homan, in the end zone, but Butkus was the deeper of the two so he just lobbed the ball toward him. Chris Hanburger, the ubiquitous Washington linebacker, leaped for the ball, but it was too high for him to reach. Butkus leaped (if you can call the jump of a 6′3″, 245-pounder a leap), too, and he pulled the ball into his chest for the winning point.

An official at first dropped a flag, indicating an ineligible receiver, but Butkus quickly reminded him he had reported into the game as an eligible receiver.

"I've never scored on a screwier play," said Butkus, who had last caught a pass twelve years before as a high school fullback. His only previous pro score came on a safety.

For the most part, though, there's nothing screwy or tricky about the plays Butkus makes. Usually, they're bone-jarring, play-stifling tackles, the kind on which the ball carrier knows at once he's been tackled, make no mistake about it.

Although there is a small collection of outstanding middle line-backers in the league, none throughout the years has been praised so consistently by friend and foe alike as Butkus has. If he played on a team that was more competitive than the Bears, he probably could at some time become the league's most valuable player. He's certainly the most valuable Bear, because without him the Bears would have little to look forward to each Sunday. As it is, their opponents don't look forward to facing Butkus on the Sundays they have to.

The comments about him read like a long list of excerpts from reviews of a hit play.

"He's the best I ever played against," says center Ken Iman of the Los Angeles Rams. "He's so big and strong and quick. He likes to punish people. You have to block him viciously. If you don't, he'll push you all over the field."

A few years ago, while the Pittsburgh Steelers were still more of

the league's patsies than the Bears, Terry Hanratty found out what it was like to have Butkus push him all over the field.

"I think he's the greatest football player I've ever faced," the quarterback said, surprised that he was still alive to tell about it. "He's the total defensive player. He makes most of his tackles before the runner reaches the line of scrimmage. He's in on most of the line tackles and he still handles his roaming job behind the line."

Hanratty then went on to explain how Butkus forced him into the first safety he had ever suffered. "I was going to try a little flat pass to the left," he related, "but when I took one step that way, Butkus was already two steps into the backfield so I had to switch directions. When I tried to reverse my steps to get rid of the pass, I was nailed by someone else. That's really a blow to the ego. It's like Wilt Chamberlain missing a dunk shot."

Tommy Prothro didn't get to see too much of Butkus while he coached the Rams, but he saw enough to say that "Dick Butkus is a legendary football player. He looks fat, clumsy and awkward, but he kicks the devil out of everybody and if you pass, he's right there."

That's one of the things that amazes football people about Butkus. Not only does he cause an offense all sorts of chaos at the line or in the backfield, but he also fouls up a team's plans on short- and medium-length passes by backpedaling into the coverage as if he were Rudolf Nureyev on stage.

"He's all around the ball, all the time," says Alex Karras, himself an outstanding defensive player when he was with Detroit. "He's very aggressive and brutal. He'll beat you up. He's a wild, wild performer. If you had eleven Butkuses going against you, you wouldn't get any points on the scoreboard ever."

Not everyone is enamored of Butkus's play. He has had a feud going for several seasons with Karras's old team, which feels it has an excellent linebacker in Mike Lucci, who they believe is unfairly over-shadowed by all the tumult that surrounds Butkus. But the Lions' feeling goes even beyond that. "He's a dirty player, no matter what anyone says," General Manager Russ Thomas has stated.

Butkus, however, resents the suggestion that anything he does is dirty. It's all done in the good clean fun of professional football, he insists.

"I wouldn't ever set out to hurt anybody deliberately," he once said in a television interview, "unless it was, you know, important, like a league game or something."

On another TV show, he said his favorite movie was *Hush, Hush, Sweet Charlotte* because a scene in which a head comes rolling down a flight of stairs prompts a scene in his own mind in which he decapitates a quarterback and watches the head bounce down the field (between the uprights, no doubt).

That, of course, was only a joke, Butkus said, just as it was a figment of someone's imagination that he once bit a referee during a game. "If I'd of been dumb enough to bite a referee," he said, "I'd have bitten his arm off."

No matter how much he protests or denies certain of his alleged actions and behavior, Butkus can't rid himself of a tag that was given him early in his football life—The Animal.

"If they call you an animal during a game, that's fine," he says. "I can accept that. But they carry it off the field. That stuff gets kind of old."

Going all the way back to Butkus' birth, though, one finds he was animalish even then. He weighed 13 pounds when he became a large part of his Chicago Lithuanian family. He also has four brothers who were big at birth and who are big now—6-2, 225; 6-3, 200; 6-4, 275; 6-6, 235. It seems the five Butkus brothers could make an awesome defense by themselves.

But Dick is the only one who became a professional football player. In fact, everything he did from grade school on was with that aim in mind.

"In the fifth grade I knew what I was going to be—a professional football player," he says. "I worked hard at becoming one, just like society says you should. It said you had to be fierce. I was fierce."

Butkus also was aware of where to start on the road to the pros. Instead of attending high school near his home, he traveled five miles across town to a vocational school where the football team was coached by a man reputed to be one of the best in the city.

"In practice," says Bernie O'Brien, a Notre Dame graduate, "he was always the hardest worker on the field."

When Butkus decided to go to the University of Illinois, he had several reasons, but one of them was that the Big Ten was probably the best place to prepare for the pros. As far as Dick was concerned, he was going to college because that's how one reached the NFL. The academic side of Illinois was only incidental.

"I just wanted to play ball and work out and they start hitting me with this homework business," he once said. But he survived the ordeal and achieved his ambition when the Bears selected him in the first round of the 1965 draft.

"The minute I looked at the guy in training camp, I started packing my suitcase," says Bill George, who had been the Bears' middle linebacker for more than a decade.

Probably no rookie ever came into the NFL with more ability and more prepared to take over a job. As in his earlier stages of development, football was all that mattered and he was caught up in it completely from the minute he emerged from the locker room.

"I used to take the pre-game warmups just as seriously as the games," he has written in his book, *Stop Action.* "I never smiled, goofed off or even talked to anyone. I used to look at the other team just to try and catch some guy smiling or laughing and I'd use that to get myself worked up."

During a game Butkus *always* is worked up, crashing here, bulling his way there, always in a frenzy.

"When I'm playing," he says, "I can get myself excited over almost nothing and reach a peak quickly. It doesn't take much for me to get teed off. Sometimes I make some of it up—if a guy looks at me the wrong way."

Furthermore, Butkus says he invents feuds to get himself up for a game. All he needs is to hear something or read something or see something that might in the least little way be anything but 150 percent flattering to him or his team.

This is the angry side of Butkus. There's another side and this is just as dangerous for Chicago opponents. It's Butkus's ability to "read" plays and quarterbacks and determine beforehand where the ball is going.

"I enjoy that part of the game as much as any, the finesse and strategy that is as much a part of the game as the bodily contact," says Butkus, who calls defensive signals. "If it was just matching strength, the strongest man would win every time. It's also being smart enough to maneuver players and teams into situations where you can use your strength against their weakness."

Butkus's powers of observation are as potent as his powers of destruction. He watches the quarterback's mouth when he's in the huddle and he watches his feet when he's behind the center.

By watching the mouth, Butkus sometimes can read the quarterback's lips and pick up the play or at least the count. For example, he says, he had little trouble picking up plays that were called by Joe Kapp and Milt Plum.

By watching the feet, Butkus sometimes can get an idea of which way the play is going. "If a quarterback's feet are even, he's going to go one way," Butkus writes. "If his left foot is back, he's going to go that way. If the right foot is back, he's going to drop back. Some of them even drop back differently depending on which way they're going to throw the ball. It just takes experience and a quarterback who doesn't study his own moves on the game films."

Some quarterbacks, however, have the feeling that no matter how much they study themselves on film, Butkus has studied them more closely, and no matter what they try to do to avoid him, he's going to be there anyway.

Mike Curtis

Perhaps it all began when he was three years old. "My mother and father told me I used to put baby chickens in a milk bottle and then crush them to death with a stick," Mike Curtis says. And then it blossomed a little more when he was five. "I had this thing about melting crayons on radiators," he recalls. "I'd take a fresh box of crayons and press them against a hot radiator until they melted. I got some kind of kick out of watching them melt and run down on the floor. My parents spanked my behind every time I did it, but I thought they looked sort of neat. Our radiators always looked like Christmas trees."

There have been many times, many years later, that grown men— very grown men—have come away from confrontations with Mike Curtis feeling like those crushed baby chicks or those melted crayons. They haven't had to scrape Jim Plunkett, for example, out of the bottom of a milk bottle or off a radiator, but perhaps he sometimes wonders why not.

"Just looking at that guy across the line of scrimmage scares you a little," the young New England quarterback says. "He is tough, he hits and when he does, he puts everything into it. I like to stay away from that guy as much as possible the way he gambles and blitzes."

No one in the same stadium with the Baltimore middle linebacker is safe. Opposing players aren't safe; neither are his own teammates. Not even fans are safe. Donald Ennis found that out one Saturday afternoon in Baltimore's Memorial Stadium.

Ennis, a 30-year-old Colt fan, had traveled to Baltimore by bus from Rochester, New York, to watch the Colts play the Miami Dolphins in an important late-season game. With about three minutes remaining and Baltimore leading 14–3, Ennis got a crazy idea in his head. He was going to run onto the field and grab the football off the ground while the Baltimore defense and the Miami offense huddled.

Ennis did run onto the field and he did scoop up the ball, but he didn't get any farther than running backs who stray into Curtis's area. The Colt they call "Animal" whacked Ennis, and the foolhardy adventurer wound up, first on the ground, then at the police station and finally in the hospital.

"Curtis went out of his way to get me," said Ennis, who suffered pinched nerves and a bruised hip and spine. "He circled his linemen and came after me. I didn't even see him coming."

Ennis could easily have been any one of a number of ball carriers talking about a play in a game. Frequently, the player with the ball is thumped to the ground by this man he didn't see coming. But why would a 6'2", 232-pound professional football player pounce on a hapless civilian?

"I saw him pick up the ball and I said what the hell's going on here?" Curtis explained. "He shouldn't have been on the field at all. This happens all over the country and the cops don't stop it. But when he comes in my area and I'm the last man, I'm going to get him. I didn't try to hurt him. I bumped him to get the football. If I wanted to hurt him, he would have been carried off the field."

Terry Bradshaw hasn't needed help to get off the field after an encounter with Curtis, but he knows how Ennis felt. "He and I ran into each other head-on," the 6'3", 214-pound quarterback says, "and he stung me pretty good."

When Mike Curtis stings, it's not like a bee, but rather like a pile driver. On every play he unleashes his entire body force against the object of his pursuit, and most of the time it doesn't matter whether that object is wearing the same uniform as he is or a different one.

Once, in practice, he tackled fullback Terry Cole so viciously that Don Shula, then the Baltimore coach, banished him to the sideline to cool off for forty-five minutes. Don McCafferty, who succeeded Shula, never gave Curtis that type of treatment, but he often winced when Mike flung his body against an offensive Colt.

"Mike can be dangerous to our own people sometimes," McCafferty said once. "He gets teed off at his own teammates in practice if he thinks they made a mistake or loafed. It's good that he goes out 100 percent all the time, but if everybody did, we wouldn't have enough bodies for the game on Sunday."

At times, it was said, Curtis even gave John Unitas, the most important person in Baltimore's championship plans, the 100-percent treatment. Curtis, however, insisted he didn't rough up Unitas. "I never really hit him hard," he said. "I growl at him and bite him a little bit, that's all."

Curtis smiled when he said that, just as he might eventually smile to indicate he's putting on somebody who wants to hear him tell what a savage animal he really is. In his earlier days as an all-pro linebacker, Curtis willingly fed the image that had been built around him. That kind of publicity, he reasoned, couldn't hurt. His agent even went so far as to put out a brochure intended to attract job or endorsement offers. "This man is a GENTLEMAN!" the brochure began. "He is also . . . an ANIMAL!"

But once he had achieved the notoriety he sought, he tended to play down the animal image. "I'm no animal," he says. "I am aggresssive, very aggressive, but I'm not an animal. They say I go berserk on the field. I don't think that's exactly true. I've never tried to hurt anybody. I've never hit low for the legs or anything like that. It's just that I love contact. I don't want to hurt anybody, because I want them to stay in the game and come back and hit."

Nevertheless, Curtis continues to be recognized as a savage tackler, one whose presence soon becomes felt by ball carriers even at times when he might not be around. Even his teammates recognize the kind of player Curtis is.

"Mike is the most vicious football player I've ever seen," Billy Ray Smith, a former Baltimore defensive lineman, once said. To which another Baltimore Smith, Bubba, added later, "Mike has got to be the naturally meanest man on the field. He may be the meanest man in the world."

Ironically, Curtis nearly missed getting a chance to be "the meanest man in the world." The Colts' No. 1 draft choice in 1965, the Duke graduate was a fullback before he became a linebacker. But he was a third-string fullback and in that first season, he ran the ball six times and gained a net total of one yard and he caught one pass for 5 yards. The following season he was switched to linebacker, where he filled in at an outside spot. In 1967, when he was ready to erupt into his own, he suffered a knee injury, underwent surgery and played only three games.

Thus, it wasn't until 1968 that he finally had his first full year as a starting linebacker, but he immediately let everyone know how good he was because he made all-pro that season. That, however, was also the season that made him more upset than he ever had been as a football player.

That was the season the Colts won thirteen of their fourteen regular-season games and two playoff contests, then suffered a humiliating loss to the New York Jets in the Super Bowl.

"It's hard to forget that," Curtis said long afterward. "It made a helluva impression on us. We walked over everyone during the season and we beat all the big teams. When we got to Miami, there was sort of a carnival atmosphere. Wives and girl friends were there with us and there wasn't a curfew until just before the game. And I don't think we had the proper respect for the AFL."

Curtis was so intense during that game that when Earl Morrall failed to see Jimmy Orr, who was wide open in scoring position, on the last play of the first half and instead threw to Jerry Hill only to have the pass intercepted, he ran onto the field cursing and shaking his fist at Morrall.

"I couldn't believe it," Curtis said later. "I just couldn't believe it. But there it was, the whole tragic, stupid loss summed up in that one lousy play. Everyone could see Orr out there by himself. Everyone but Earl. My behavior was irrational, but the game was like a bad dream. No one knows the despair, the abject humiliation the Colts felt. We were a perfect football machine and we were the first National Football League team to lose the Super Bowl."

Curtis would have done anything to get back to the Super Bowl following the 1969 season, but he and the Colts had to wait two years to try and polish their damaged prestige and repair their wounded psyche. In the meantime, Curtis again switched positions, this time to middle line-backer. It happened midway through the 1969 season and while Curtis lost his status as an all-pro outside linebacker he nevertheless gained by the switch.

"I like it better in the middle," he said after trying it. "It's a lot busier, but you don't get as tired. There are a lot of people around all the time, going this way and that, and you don't have to run nearly as far to get them."

In addition, Curtis's desire for hitting people was fulfilled more in the middle because the man in the middle is in on more plays and therefore gets an opportunity to make more tackles. In other words, it gave Curtis the chance to impress upon ball carriers more frequently how savage he really could be.

Hank Bullough was the Colts' linebacker coach when Curtis made the switch and he was impressed with how his student always strived to be a perfectionist. "He wants to play a perfect game some day," Bullough said. "He wants to make every tackle, stuff every blocker and knock down every pass. It can't be done, but Mike actually strives to accomplish it."

Curtis's fervor in his first full year at the new position helped the Colts get back to the Super Bowl following the 1970 season. It also helped them win the game with a 16–13 decisoin over Dallas on Jim O'Brien's field goal with five seconds left.

The Colts awarded two game balls afterward, one to O'Brien and one to Coach Don McCafferty, and Chuck Howley, a Dallas linebacker, was awarded a car as the game's outstanding player. Thus, Curtis was virtually overlooked despite the fact that he helped force a fumble from Duane Thomas at the one-yard line in the third quarter, thereby preventing what would have been the winning score for the Cowboys, and he intercepted a Craig Morton pass with fifty-nine seconds to go, setting up O'Brien's field goal.

But Curtis wasn't upset over the lack of recognition. He had entered the game with one goal, and that was to win so he could get a Super Bowl ring. "That's what I wanted, the Super Bowl ring," he says. "It represents accomplishment. The money ($15,000) is only icing on the cake and you can buy a car any place. But you can't buy a Super Bowl ring. You got to win it."

If Curtis was different in that he didn't care about such things as money and a car, it wasn't surprising because he is an unusual person among pro football players. He's an individual in all respects and he isn't reluctant to show it. For example, he was the first name player to report to camp in 1970 during the player-management labor dispute and he was the first player to drop out of the Players Association, a step he took in 1972. Furthermore, he doesn't hang around with his teammates much and he believes players should follow the coach's orders and accept the rigid discipline inherent in the game.

"If I was a coach, I'd be like Patton," says Curtis, who saw the movie of the same name more than half a dozen times. "I'd want my players to be as obedient as Patton's soldiers. I would have made a good soldier. I follow orders. I'm not always asking questions."

Curtis's teammates never have resented his attitude or his desire to be a loner or his feeling about not striking when they did and not belonging to the union when they do. They respect his beliefs and his behavior. They especially appreciate his behavior on the field.

"I don't know what causes Mike to be like he is," says Bubba Smith, "but it's nice to have that crazy dude on our side."

Willie Lanier

More than one thousand men of sizes large, larger and largest play in the National Football League each year, so it isn't always easy for one player to recall all the others he's played against. Larry Brown, however, remembers Willie Lanier as well as he remembers what he ate for breakfast this morning. Brown knows him from the first time the Washington Redskins met the Kansas City Chiefs.

"Lanier really worked me over," says Brown of that game in 1971 when the Chiefs halted Washington's six-game winning streak. "It got so bad out there that I was going through a hole and then looking down the line wondering where that damned guy was coming from next. Wow! I told him afterwards that as far as I was concerned I wouldn't even fly over their new stadium in an airplane."

When Willie Lanier hits people, it feels as if the hit was made by a bomb that was dropped from an airplane. In that game with Washington, the first time Brown got the ball, Lanier belted him, forcing the ball out of his grasp and his senses out of his head. The Chiefs' middle linebacker recovered Brown's fumble, setting up Kansas City's first score, and the next time the Redskins got the ball he intercepted a Bill Kilmer pass, halting a Washington threat.

A week earlier, John Fuqua, a rugged Pittsburgh running back, had the misfortune to run into Lanier—more than once. In fact, Lanier hit him so often and so hard that late in the game Fuqua was open for a pass from Terry Bradshaw, but he turned and looked to see where Lanier was. The result was Fuqua dropped the ball even though Lanier wasn't in the area and the road to the end zone was open.

To climax a period of particularly indicative play, one week after the Washington contest Lanier turned in another superb effort against Oakland that helped knock the Raiders out of the playoffs for the first time in five years. The game, as the outcome showed, turned on one play.

With time running out, the Raiders were only thirty-six inches away from winning the game, but Coach John Madden decided to settle for a tying field goal instead of trying for a winning touchdown. He based his decision on the results of the third-down play on which Lanier blocked Don Highsmith's burst for the goal line. Asked after the game why he didn't make it, Highsmith replied, "When I got there, I met Lanier."

Numerous ball carriers have met Lanier and none find the introduction very social or very enjoyable. What Lanier was found to be, though, was the best middle linebacker in the league that season, the first time such a distinction went to a black player. The distinction is all the more impressive when it's realized that a black middle linebacker is only slightly less rare in the NFL than a black quarterback.

For Lanier to reach that stature, he had to have two important ingredients—his own ability and determination and the enlightened practices of his coach, Hank Stram.

Actually, there was a third ingredient, a scouting friend of Stram's who tipped off the coach about Lanier.

"Lanier was drafted in 1967, the year Bob Hyland [a Boston College center] made such a big name for himself," Stram says. "I asked this scouting friend of mine who he thought was the No. 1 prospect in the East."

"You may think I'm crazy," the friend said, "but there's a kid at Morgan State who's the best at his position I've ever seen."

"What impressed me about that," Stram says, "is that this came from a guy who almost never praised anybody. He told me, 'This kid destroys people.'"

So the Chiefs drafted Lanier in the second round, and the Clover, Virginia, native signed with them, knowing he had a chance to become a rare species, a black man in the middle.

"I was very much aware that there weren't any blacks at that posi-

Dick Butkus: The buck stops here.

Tommy Nobis: Reception committee.

Mike Lucci: The anchor.

Nick Buoniconti: Attorney for the defense.

en Dawson: Looking for the edge.

(left)
Mr. Csonka, meet Mr. Lanier.

(right)
Bob Griese: Over the top.

Mike Lucci: "If only that guy were Butkus."

nton: Moving the purple people-eaters.

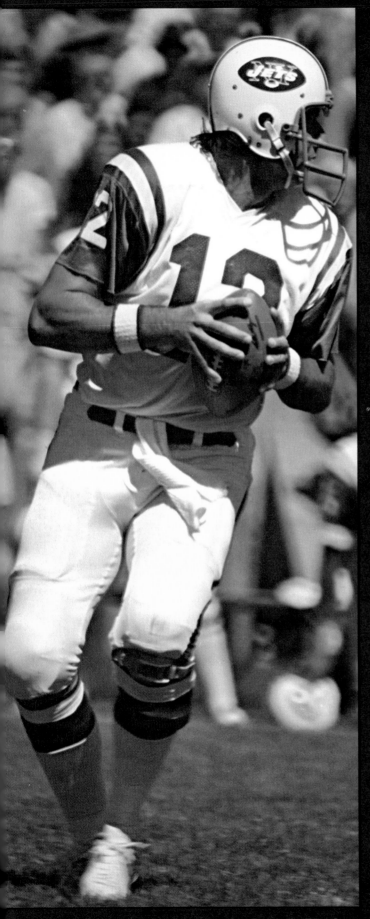

Joe Namath: The Arm.

Part of a crowd.

Alone in a crowd.

Fran Tarkenton: Hitting the open man.

Jack Ham: Watch for us this year.

tion just like I was aware there were no black quarterbacks," recalls the 6'1", 245-pounder who's affectionately known to his teammates as Honey Bear. "So when I got to the Chiefs' camp and they switched me to the outside, I said to myself, 'What is this?'"

But Lanier was willing to wait and see how things developed rather than accuse Stram of the football form of racial prejudice. "You have to consider that such a change can be for innocent reasons," Lanier says. "Perhaps the coach believes—without any reference to race—that it would be best for the team, that it would help you win. So you have to be extra patient and wait a little longer and see."

Lanier didn't have to wait long. Stram soon planted him in the middle and he has grown there ever since. What made the coach's decision even more intriguing was that he selected Lanier over Jim Lynch, a fierce tackler who had been an All-American at Notre Dame. Furthermore, Lynch was white.

"Either one of them could've played the middle," Stram explains. "Both of them are highly intelligent football players and have outstanding physical ability. Since Lanier is bigger than Lynch it seemed we'd be better off using him in the middle. We had had trouble before with people running up the middle on us. I knew they wouldn't do that with Lanier there."

Lanier, who may be the most articulate of the middle linebackers generally considered to be the best in the league, recalls that he was highly skeptical of the opportunity he would receive but admits it turned out that he was overly skeptical. He also recalls the pressure he felt once he got the full-fledged opportunity he wanted.

"There was quite a bit of pressure in my rookie year," he says. "It was an individual thing that made me approach the situation from the standpoint that I was the first and therefore how I did would either help others to play the position or, if I didn't make it, well, then maybe it would be a while before someone else got the opportunity. It was a case of what is it, what do you have to do, are you setting the stage for other black ballplayers who would like to be middle linebackers? Consequently, there was pressure."

Lanier, however, overcame the pressure, gained the starting job in the fourth game of his rookie (1967) season and has held it ever since. Ever since, that is, except for the games he missed that first year because of a head injury.

Lanier, it seems, learned in high school that the best way to tackle the ball carrier was with his head. "I'd sort of lock my neck so I wouldn't get whiplash and aim my head at the runner." he says. "It took me a while, but I finally learned that teaching players to use their head in tackling is wrong. You should think with your head instead of using it as a weapon."

But before he became enlightened about the proper use of his head, Lanier ran into various problems—head first, of course.

"I was just starting at middle linebacker and I wanted to prove the coach's decision to start me was a valid one so I was trying to play very aggressively," Lanier says, remembering a game against San Diego. "I was trying to tackle Brad Hubbert when I got hurt. I dove across a guard and was in mid-air. The first thing that hit Hubbert's leg was my head. In a situation like that, you're going to absorb the whole force of the blow on the point of impact, which was my head."

But a mild concussion didn't knock any sense into Lanier's head and he kept using it to make tackles. Later in the season he collapsed during a game with Denver and still later, in a second game against San Diego, he went to tackle John Hadl only to find that there were two John Hadls.

"I tackled the one that was the vision," Lanier relates, "and then I said to myself, 'I'm getting the hell out of here' and I went off the field."

From there, Lanier went to the Mayo Clinic for tests and he came away with advice to use something other than his head. That something turned out to be shoulders and arms, four weapons that Lanier has used with reckless abandon and great success ever since.

"He's the best middle linebacker I've ever played against," says Jon Morris, New England's center.

"There's no better middle linebacker in football," echoes running back Mike Garrett of San Diego.

Buck Buchanan, Willie's 6'8" teammate, says he'll play pro football as long as Lanier does. "When he quits playing, that'll be the end of my career, too," says the defensive tackle. "Willie not only cuts off sweeps, he cuts off everything. He just stops the whole team."

Larry Csonka, one of the most bruising runners in the game, has had enough meetings with Lanier to know him intimately. "It's bad enough running into a grizzly bear," the Miami back remarks. "But it's murder when he's a smart grizzly."

Csonka, however, was the key figure in a play that proved that even smart grizzly bears aren't infallible. It happened in the 1971 play-off game between Kansas City and Miami, the longest pro game ever played. The Dolphins won it, 27—24, and Csonka's 29-yard run set up Garo Yepremian's winning field goal in the second overtime period. The play called for Bob Griese, the quarterback, and Jim Kiick, a running back, to start to the right while Csonka went left and took a handoff from Griese. For the play to work, the middle linebacker has to go for the fake and that's exactly what Lanier did.

"I followed Kiick and as soon as I had taken a step and a half to the outside I said to myself, 'Damn, the play is going the other way.' The reason the play worked so well was that Griese hadn't shown it to us before. At that particular time of the game, there was a certain tenseness you ordinarily wouldn't be confronted with. It was a time of immediate choice and we were keyed to react to what the Dolphins had showed us in the past."

The reason Griese went to that play, though, was because Lanier and his fellow linebackers had done such a brilliant job of stopping the Miami running game the rest of the day. By that time, Lanier already had made 13 tackles, assisted on 9 others and intercepted a pass.

Despite the extremely frustrating loss, Lanier was able to appreciate the event for what it was, which is a good indication of the attitude he has for the game.

"I really enjoyed playing it," Willie says. "I never had so much fun playing a football game in my whole career. It's hard to describe to anyone who hasn't experienced it—the feeling of a sudden death, the pressure that's involved, the concentration that's necessary and the way you really have to totally perform because you realize that any mistake you make can be the game-winning mistake, and it's the thing that really heightens your normal insight into the contest. From that standpoint, it was a tremendous contest. I can look back for a long time and savor it. I participated in the longest game ever—82 minutes and 40 seconds. I'll never forget it. Very few people can have an experience like that."

Nor do many people take the time and expend the energy to experience the satisfaction of working with young people, especially those who are extremely poor and perhaps headed in a questionable direction. But Willie has spent hours and hours of his non-playing time speaking to youth groups, especially on the subject of drug abuse.

"I make personal appearances and speeches on a non-fee basis," he explains, "so that I might be able to assist various youth organizations because I feel this is something I should do for the younger people who want to get started in sports and want to meet ballplayers but ordinarily wouldn't have the opportunity to do so."

In serving kids in this way, Lanier is simply extending his on-field leadership qualities to endeavors off the field. Once Lanier became entrenched in his job on the field with the Chiefs, it became obvious that he also was assuming the role of the defensive leader.

Never was this role more vividly displayed than in the Chiefs' playoff game against the New York Jets in 1969. The Jets were trailing, 6–3, but behind the mastery of Joe Namath they had moved to the Kansas City one-yard line where they had a first down.

"Willie was crying on the goal line," cornerback Emmitt Thomas recalls. "He was hysterical. He kept begging us to stop them. He said we had worked since July for this and we couldn't throw it away in one series."

The Jets came out of their huddle and as they lined up, one voice was heard above everything else.

"Dammit," Lanier screamed, "they're not going to score."

The Jets did score but only a field goal, and the Chiefs went on to score a touchdown themselves, win the game and advance to the Super Bowl, where they beat the Minnesota Vikings.

Mike Lucci

"I guess," Mike Lucci once said, "I'm just a loud-mouthed middle linebacker."

Even without the admission, that fact has become evident throughout the years Lucci has been playing for the Detroit Lions. Take these outbursts, for example:

"If the Vikings go all the way," he said one time in a discussion of Minnesota, a division rival, "it'll be another 1963, when the Bears did it the same way, without an offense. The Vikings have a crummy offense."

Speaking of Hank Stram, Kansas City's coach, he said, "He's an egotistical midget among the giants. He's the King Tut."

What he said to an official during a game with Green Bay isn't printable, but the words were clear enough to the official because he threw Lucci out of the game.

The dispute arose over a touchdown the official awarded Donny Anderson who had plunged across the middle trying to cover the one yard necessary for the score. Lucci was one of the Lion defenders who stopped Anderson, and he argued that the Packer back never reached the goal line.

Whipping off his helmet, Lucci jumped up and down, stuck his chin right in the official's face and then flung his helmet to the ground.

Lucci had the rest of the afternoon to calm down, but his anger skyrocketed again later in the week when he learned Commissioner Pete Rozelle had fined him $300 for his behavior.

"I'm not complaining about being thrown out of the game," the angry young Lion said, "but the fine's a little stiff and there are some things I don't like about it. It's a matter of principle." He argued that the standard fine for being ejected was supposed to be $50 and said that was the amount he was fined when he was kicked out of a game with Pittsburgh two years earlier.

Football officials, however, aren't the only people who incur Lucci's wrath. When he plays for the Lions' off-season basketball team, Lucci frequently bellows at the officials in that game, too. "Put a striped shirt on them and they're all the same," he growls. "It's their attitude. They all think they're so important."

Lucci has so much to say about so many people because he speaks like he plays—emotionally.

"I am an emotional man, I admit it," he says. "Football is a very emotional game, of course, and I probably get carried away with it more than most guys. It's the only way I know how to play. I love the game. I enjoy everything that goes with it. I enjoy the hitting and the crowds and beating the other team. When we hit the field and I see the other team, the other colors, the people there, I'm ready. I enjoy beating the other guy. I like to hit people and there is a certain excitement in the sport."

As emotional as he is in other situations, though, Lucci saves his most fervent emotion for one man, one object. His name is Dick Butkus.

Emotion runs high in Lucci and in Detroit when the name Butkus is mentioned. Butkus also happens to be a middle linebacker and he happens to play in the same division as Lucci. He also happens to have received more acclaim over the years than Lucci.

"He was the player rep for Chicago when I was the rep for Detroit," Lucci recalls. "We got to be pretty friendly. We bounced around a little together and had a few drinks."

It was inevitable, though, that the friendship would be overcome by the conflict inherent in the situation. It's the nature of the beast, and they soon were ripping into each other, with some outside assistance, as if they were fighting to see who was the king of the jungle.

"It all started one year before we played the Bears," Lucci says. "There were a lot of big articles on Butkus and me, and Joe Schmidt [then the Detroit coach] came out and said I was the best one in the division. That came out in a Detroit paper and then a Chicago writer got into the act and before they got through with it I was quoted as saying Butkus was overrated and so on.

"What I did say, kind of jokingly [and kind of not], was that Butkus got his share of publicity and they made a big deal out of it. The upshot was that Butkus made a grumpy statement to the effect that 'why didn't he [Lucci] try to play his way into the Pro Bowl instead of talking his way into it.'"

Butkus's reference to the Pro Bowl stemmed from the situation in 1969 where Lucci had his finest season as a pro but was not selected for the All-Star game. Butkus was. Joe Schmidt was particularly incensed over the slight.

"It's a damn shame," said the coach who was the prototype for the middle linebacker as the position is played today. "We are second on defense, we had three shutouts, we won five games more than last season and we got only one guy picked from our defense. I'm disturbed that Lucci wasn't picked. I don't know why he wasn't. The coaches pick the Pro Bowl players and there's a lot of politics involved in the selections."

It didn't help Schmidt's lack of understanding of the situation that

the Bears won only one game that season. Lucci didn't appreciate the situation either.

"What bugs me," Lucci said, "is that once a guy like Butkus makes all-pro and starts getting picked for the Pro Bowl, nobody else gets a thought. Butkus could have a lousy year and he'd still be all-pro. It becomes a matter of habit by the selectors. They just automatically write down Dick Butkus. I'm not saying he doesn't deserve it; he's one of the greatest. But maybe I'm just as good."

Lucci also has been irked because he feels Butkus is called for fewer penalties than other players simply because he is Butkus. "I think the league is selling something," he says. "They're selling stars and he's one. It's not a conscious thing, but Butkus doesn't get called the same way as others."

The running feud reached its most fiery point when Butkus's book, *Stop-Action,* was published. Some of Butkus's most incendiary words were reserved for the Bears in general and Lucci in particular.

"I think they are a lot of jerks," Butkus wrote of the Lions, "from the owner, the general manager, the coach on down. Even the announcers must be a bunch of fags. If we were voting for a jerk team or organization, they'd have my vote all the way."

Getting down to individuals, Butkus said: "For the last couple of years now this Lucci has been trying to make some sort of a reputation for himself by knocking me. I wish to hell he would try to make the Pro Bowl on the field instead of with his mouth. . . . No one but those jerks has ever called me a dirty player. . . . They started this thing. Coach Joe Schmidt popping off about Lucci, how great he is."

Lucci, of course, was asked to respond to Butkus's flattering statements and he said, "I didn't know Butkus could write. I'd tell you my reaction, but you couldn't put it in the paper anyway."

The feud, however, wasn't simply on paper or a lot of words. Butkus and Lucci made that obvious before a Chicago-Detroit game when, as team captains, they met at the middle of the field for the pre-game coin toss. This traditional tableau usually shows the captains shaking hands, but that little formality was absent on this occasion.

"He didn't extend his hand," Lucci explained, "and I didn't extend mine." Did Lucci think Butkus was trying to psyche him? "If he was, it didn't work too well, did it?"

Not on that day it didn't. In sparking the Lions to a 28–3 victory over the bears, the 6'2", 235-pound Lucci intercepted three passes, racing 27 yards with one for a touchdown. The Detroit defense also sacked quarterback Bobby Douglass eight times, which equaled the team's entire output for the previous nine games.

"I wanted to show them there's another linebacker out there," Lucci said.

Everyone noticed, of course, probably even some of the Chicago fans who the year before had pelted Lucci with rotten fruit and loud jeers. His coach noticed, too.

"I just can't say enough about Lucci," Schmidt said. "I just wish I had a roomful of guys like him. He's playing on a bad leg and a bad ankle and still gave us great effort."

Lucci first showed that kind of effort when he was growing up in the western Pennsylvania town of Ambridge, which is located in the area that produced such athletes as Joe Namath, Dick Allen and Mike Ditka. He started his college career at the University of Pittsburgh but had to take his talents elsewhere when he was expelled from Pitt during his sophomore year for infractions of university rules. Also asked to leave at the same time (although not expelled) was Ed Sharockman, who later was a defensive back for the Minnesota Vikings.

Lucci continued his studies and football playing at Tennessee and there learned the fine art of linebacking. He was impressive enough that the Cleveland Browns drafted him as a future in 1961 (when teams were permitted to draft players whose original college classes had graduated), but it was a few years into his future before he was able to gain a starting job as a linebacker: in 1964, Lucci was a member of the Browns' special team when they won the NFL championship.

It was after Lucci went to the Lions in a three-team trade that he started making his mark at the job he now holds. Schmidt, the Lions' middle linebacker when Lucci arrived in Detroit in 1965, retired at the end of that season. The newcomer couldn't have hoped for a better break or a better teacher.

Besides helping him improve his linebacking play, Schmidt also eventually began giving Lucci additional leadership responsibility, first appointing him defensive co-captain with tackle Alex Karras and then giving him the job all by himself. In Lucci's mind, he adapted to the job naturally.

"I think when you're calling defenses, you sort of assume the leader-

ship role because you're running things," he says. "It just goes from there. You don't say, 'I'm going to be the leader, I'm going to do something.' If you believe something, you have to say it. If you have to do something, you do it. You can lead by example or you can lead by just being the person you are."

Lucci is the kind of person who never gives up on a play or a game, who is aggressive and who can stir himself and his teammates into the necessary psychological frame of mind for the important games. Butkus is considered rougher than Lucci, but the Lion whose detractors call him "Lucy" has excellent pursuit and lateral movement that has helped him become one of the most feared pass defenders among linebackers.

"Lucci isn't one of the top ones physically," says Bill Nelsen, recently retired quarterback of the Browns. "But he does a fantastic job. He's strong against both the run and the pass and he's excellent in coordinating the defense."

As much as he loves to hit people and knock them loose from the ball, Lucci relishes the battles of minds that constantly takes place on each side of the line, the quarterback and the middle linebacker trying to outwit each other.

"A quarterback is trying to call the offensive play that will work against the defense," Lucci says. "I'm trying to pull a defense to stop him. In calling defensive signals, you think about the quarterback's tendencies —what he has done in the past, what he likes to do in certain situations. You're trying to outsmart him. It's sort of a game played within a game."

Sometimes one or the other loses the personal game because in trying to outsmart the foe, he outsmarts himself. It happens to everyone at one time or another.

"There was a game once where we had a definite tip on a certain pass play," Lucci relates. "Every time I saw the tip, I audibled into the correct defense. But this last time, I figured they were showing me the tip just to sucker me. They couldn't possibly run the same play again. But they did and the damn pass went for a touchdown. You feel pretty bad about something like that."

Lucci, however, doesn't feel bad too often. Usually, it's the other guy who feels bad after Lucci has hit him—physically or verbally.

Tommy Nobis

It's fortunate for the United States space exploration program that astronaut Frank Borman was a better spaceman than he was a football recruiter. Borman, for sure, was one of the extraordinarily talented men who put space rockets into orbit and spacemen on the moon. But he couldn't put Tommy Nobis in a Houston Oiler football uniform.

Borman tried, heaven knows he tried—from somewhere near the heavens. On December 8, 1965, after the two warring football leagues held their drafts, Borman was whipping around the universe in his Gemini 7 space capsule when he asked the space communications center to relay a message for him (Bell Telephone doesn't make long distance calls from *that* distance).

"Tell Nobis to sign with Houston," Borman said.

Not "One small step for man, one giant step for mankind;" not "all systems are go;" not "T minus 15 and counting," but "Tell Nobis to sign with Houston."

Now if that wasn't pressure from above, no one's had pressure from above. But Tommy Nobis was a big man (6′ 2″, 235-pound big) and he had a mind of his own. A week later, Borman, who was an avid Oiler fan and whose two sons were Oiler ballboys, got the news: Nobis had signed with the Atlanta Falcons, the newest team in the National League.

"There's no joy in Mudville," moaned Borman, who nevertheless managed to keep his spaceship on course.

Borman survived the disappointment of Nobis's decision, which is almost more than Nobis can say. Disdaining a team that was to play for the American League championship in 1967, Nobis joined an outfit that was to win only six games in its first three years.

In explaining why he chose the neophyte Falcons, Nobis said, "I guess you always want to play against the best, and I thought the best players were in the NFL. I watched these teams on television and read about them and I wanted to have an opportunity to see how good they were."

That might have been his thinking all along, but the Falcons weren't part of that thinking at first.

"I didn't even know who they were," said Nobis, who first heard of the Falcons when Gene Cronin, the team's personnel director, visited him at Texas and told him the Falcons were interested in him. "I did hear they were a first-year team, but I said then that I didn't want to play for any first-year team."

He changed his mind, however, and when he started playing against the other NFL teams, the players all must have looked like the best to him because the Falcons were the worst. With one exception, that is. Right from the start, despite the lack of support, Nobis showed that he was one of the best middle linebackers in the game.

He particularly impressed Norm Van Brocklin, who then coached the Minnesota Vikings but who later, in 1968, became the Atlanta coach. "The drafting and signing of Nobis," Van Brocklin said, "gave the Falcons recognition right from the start. He provided them with stability and a reason for hope."

Van Brocklin didn't simply utter a lot of praiseworthy words about Nobis; he also gave his opinion of the youngster on his ballot for rookie of the year that season. Asked to list his first, second and third choices for the honor, Van Brocklin wrote, "1. Tommy Nobis; 2. Tommy Nobis; 3. Tommy Nobis."

It could be said that Nobis began preparing for the day when he could command that kind of respect by a decision he made before beginning high school. Living in San Antonio, which had a large Mexican-American population, Nobis was able to select the school he wanted to attend. There were no restrictions by districts.

"There were only two or three schools really preparing kids for college," explained Nobis, who grew up in a neighborhood where the Mexicans, the blacks and the whites taunted each other with "nigger" and "white trash" and "wetback." "Most of the schools were vocational schools and I knew those weren't for me. I wanted to be prepared for college."

In harboring a desire to go to college, Nobis had no delusions of becoming a scholar; college was the means by which he could become a professional football player.

"Some people say school comes first, then football," he was to say while at Texas. "With me, football comes first, then school, because football is my business, like the law student and the engineering student. They stay up nights studying and they'll be successful because they work hard

at it. Football is my business and if I study it, it's because I want to be successful at it."

It was this type of thinking that led Nobis to Jefferson High School, whose coach, Pat Shannon, had an outstanding record as a coach and as a teacher of future college players. The school was twenty miles from Nobis's home, but he considered the trip worth it.

"It was the best decision I ever made and it turned out to be my biggest one," he says. "It wasn't a real big sacrifice. Sure, I got up at six in the morning and rode a bus for an hour to be at school by eight, but a lot of other boys did it, too. I rode the bus home some evenings, but my dad often drove over and picked me up. He enjoyed watching me practice and his being there made it easier for me. I'd get home about eight thirty at night. Mother had some food for me in the stove, but by then it usually was cold. I didn't mind, though. It all paid off, in more ways than one."

When he was a sophomore at Jefferson, Nobis was a 150-pound quarterback, but then he began growing rapidly and Shannon moved him to the other side of the line, to linebacker, before his junior season. By the time he was ready for the next step in his development as a pro football player, Nobis was the object of much affection from many colleges. The affection that was mutual, though, was with Texas. And it grew and grew and grew as Nobis, game after game, helped make himself and Texas into a national power. As a sophomore, for example, he started as a linebacker on defense and also played guard on offense as the Longhorns won the national championship by winning all ten of their regular-season games and then downing Navy and Roger Staubach in the Cotton Bowl.

Texas missed a second straight national championship by one point, a 14–13 loss to Arkansas, the following season, then skidded to a mediocre 6–4 record in Nobis's senior year. But that didn't tarnish the reputation of the All-American linebacker. A picture of him, for example, hangs in the dining room of Moore-Hill Hall, the athletic dormitory on the campus. "The freshmen have to face that picture with their hands over their heart and sing 'The Eyes of Texas'," a school athletic official says. "Tommy is still remembered with a lot of respect around here."

The recollection of that last year, however, bothered Nobis. "Being part of two great teams as a sophomore and a junior and then coming up to your senior year, when you feel like it's 'your' team, and being 6 and 4 is a tremendous letdown," he says. "Sure, I was the No. 1 draft choice and

received a real attractive contract, but I couldn't enjoy it like I had hoped I would because of what I was leaving behind at the university.

"Maybe the good Lord was getting me ready for what was ahead at Atlanta. I've kinda joked about it, but things really changed from my senior year on."

Things changed more on a team level than on a personal level, but Nobis nevertheless learned that these guys in the pros weren't quite the lambs he faced in college.

"I guess you might say that my real introduction to the pros, my welcome to the club, came in our second game against the Philadelphia Eagles," the Texan relates. "On the first play of the game, one of their tackles, Bob Brown, a big, mean, tough, sonuvagun, caught me looking the wrong way and nailed me with a perfect block. Man, all I remember is seeing my feet going over my head.

"As I started to get up, Brown said, 'It's going to be a long afternoon, Nobis.' I'm not sure, but I think what I said was, 'Yes sir, it sure looks that way.' They beat us, 23–10, and between Bob Brown and Jim Ringo, it was the longest afternoon of the year for me. I got racked up time and again."

That, however, was only the beginning of the great frustration Nobis suffered in playing for an expansion team. The Falcons won three and lost eleven games in his—and their—first year, they plummeted to a 1-12-1 mark the second season and they were 2-12 the third.

"Losing every week just takes the flavor out of being alive," Nobis said at one depressing point.

"I am damned tired of losing," he said at another. "I have heard every excuse in the book and I am damned tired of losing. I've been on a loser long enough. I don't think I've always done my best, and I'm not satisfied with our defense. I'm sick and tired of coming up a dime short."

Despite the feeling that spread to every large muscle of his large body, Nobis was determined to stick it out and help turn the team into a winner. He considered the prospect of being traded to a better team, but he decided he didn't want to be.

"I came to Atlanta to do a job and I want to stay until it's done," he said.

Several years later, the Falcons did indeed become legitimate contenders for their division crown. They were still a good distance from Super

Bowl status and they hadn't traveled as far as the Miami Dolphins, also a 1966 expansion team, but at least they had attained some form of respectability. And as the distance between the old Falcons and the new Falcons grew, the frustrating memories Nobis had shrunk.

"It was terribly tough playing for losing teams," Nobis says. "But I conditioned myself for that mentally from the start. People told me, 'Don't go with an expansion club.' They said I'd get my brains beat out. I figured I'd suffer about five years of losing. But I always liked challenges. And the way things went for me, the knee injuries and the problems just made me appreciate even more how much I loved football. All that time I sat out made me appreciate what it meant to me. I knew I had to get back into football."

Until he smashed through a screen of blockers in front of Dallas's Walt Garrison and collapsed to the ground in a game in 1969, Nobis hadn't missed a game with the Falcons or with Texas. But the damaged cartilage he suffered in his right knee on that play forced him to miss nine games of that season and undergo surgery after it was over.

He played in every game in 1970, although he was shaky at first while still harboring post-operative doubts, but then came 1971 and his second major knee injury—this one to the left knee in a game against St. Louis. This mishap knocked him out of ten games and touched off speculation that he might have to move to center where much less mobility is required than at middle linebacker. The Falcons, however, quickly quashed such speculation.

"I wouldn't have objected if that [a position switch] were the best thing for the team, for them and for me," Nobis said. "But it hurts to pick up the paper and read you will be switched to center because you have gimpy legs."

To suggest there was ever anything gimpy about Nobis would bring a chuckle or a look of incredulity from the people he's played against. For instance, Larry Csonka has said he would rather face Dick Butkus than Nobis. "Nobis doesn't get wild-eyed like Butkus," Miami's fine running back explained. "He keeps a coldness about him, and if you don't watch out he'll put you out of the game."

Ken Willard, San Francisco's rugged back, agrees with Csonka. *Playboy* magazine once published an article on Butkus, calling him the toughest linebacker in the game. Willard read the article and then

wrote a letter to *Playboy*. "When you get around to doing a story on the best linebacker in professional football," he wrote, "may I suggest Tommy Nobis of the Atlanta Falcons?"

The complimentary words are nice to hear, but Nobis appreciates the action more—the action of the Falcons winning games. One of the most gratifying victories came in 1972, when Atlanta was fighting for the National Conference's Western Division championship. It was a 31–3 triumph over the Los Angeles Rams, and six of the Falcons' points were scored by Nobis on a 29-yard romp with a pass interception. When he reached the end zone with his first touchdown since 1967, he wound up and fired the ball into the stands.

"I didn't know what I was going to do once I got there," he said, "but I knew I was going to do something."

"That throw," said Falcon president Frank Wall, "was letting go of seven years of frustration."

Passers

Terry Bradshaw

It was as if a methodical boxer were working on Terry Bradshaw before and during the Pittsburgh Steelers' first appearance ever in a conference championship game. First, in preparing for the game, Bradshaw got it in the stomach; then, during the game, he got it in the head.

Bradshaw, who less than a week earlier had thrown the pass on which Franco Harris made a miraculous catch and scored the winning touchdown in the playoff game against Oakland, was busily preparing for the American Conference title contest against the unbeaten Miami Dolphins when he was stricken with a stomach virus. The attack left him weak with a headache and in the hospital for two nights.

The first night he was at Pittsburgh's Divine Providence Hospital, the Thursday prior to the Sunday game, he was besieged by people asking about his health and nurses seeking his autograph. His most relaxing moments were spent in an old tub full of hot water.

"They fixed me up a bath like they do after a woman has a baby," Bradshaw related the next day. "I crawled into that hot water, stretched out, put my head back and felt great. I slept for a couple of hours, it was so great. Before that I was really hurting. But those nurses were really nice. Whatever made me feel better they tried to let me do. I was in that tub three times."

The next day at practice, a mile away at Three Rivers Stadium, Bradshaw went through a ninety-minute workout but had one interruption. "I had to come in once just to go to the bathroom," he explained before returning to the hospital for one more night and another tub full of hot water. "I don't know what I'll do Sunday if that happens."

It didn't happen Sunday, but something else did. It happened when he tried to run for a touchdown in the first quarter and was tackled and flipped upside down by Jake Scott, the Dolphins' aggressive safety.

"I don't know what happened," the quarterback said afterward, trying to recall the play. "I blanked out. I thought I was in, but I was just laying there out cold."

Bradshaw was in for three plays the next time Pittsburgh had the ball, but he didn't return again until only seven minutes remained in the game. By the time he reappeared, the 7–0 lead he had engineered had turned into a 21–10 deficit.

"I thought I knew what was going on, but I really didn't," Bradshaw said of the time he spent on the sidelines trying to realize that since it was Sunday, the Steelers must be playing Miami. "I was pretty looney. I kept looking at the plays in our game plan and they were Greek to me. They didn't look like anything we had practiced. I could have sworn the game plan was somebody else's. I kept looking at the heading to see if it was some other team's. Then Terry [Hanratty, his replacement] kept quizzing me and telling me stuff and I didn't know what he was talking about."

Of such looney situations is history made. The outcome of the game never will change and the Dolphins' 1972 record will remain un-blemished, but judging from the way Bradshaw moved the Steelers through the Miami defense the first time they had the ball and then again on the first series after he returned in the final quarter, indicate that his presence in the entire game could have been interesting.

Nevertheless, his presence in the Steeler lineup the past three years has helped make Pittsburgh an intersting club, something it rarely has been in its long history.

The Steelers have had many name quarterbacks on their roster throughout the years, such people as John Unitas, Bobby Layne, Earl Morrall, Len Dawson and Bill Nelsen. But none of these quarterbacks ever did much for the Steelers Unitas, for example, was cut before the season began; Dawson was kept on the bench for three years and Morrall was sent on his way after only a season plus a couple of games.

Steeler fans, then, couldn't be blamed for being skeptical when their favorite loser made Bradshaw the first draft selection in the NFL in 1970. On the one hand, blond Terry played college football at a small

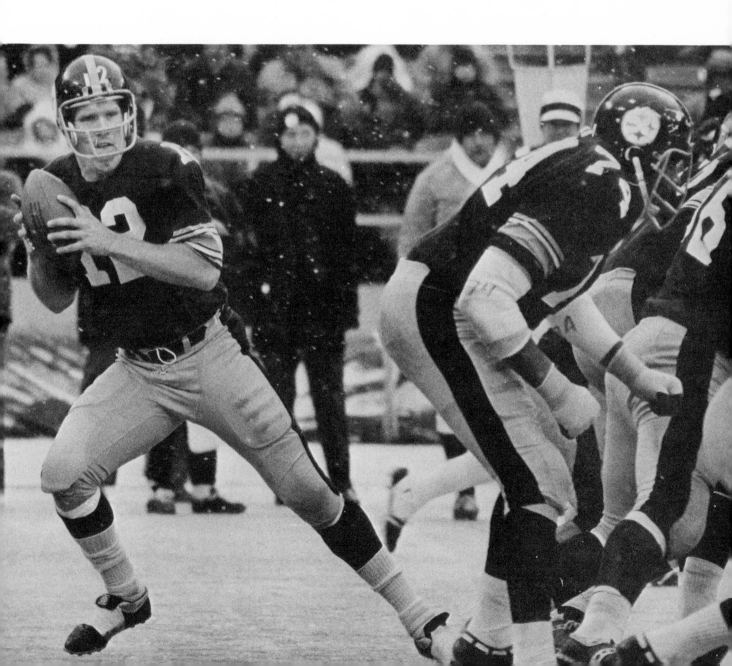

school, Louisiana Tech, and most fans weren't familiar with him even though all pro scouts were and considered him an A-1 choice. On the other hand, the fans figured, if he was as good as the scouts insisted, the Steelers would find some way to foul him up or let him go.

So imagine the fans' delight when Bradshaw played well enough in the second half of his first exhibition game to edge by Terry Hanratty into the starting job and then proceed to spark the Steelers to successive, incredible pre-season victories over Minnesota, the New York Giants, the Boston Patriots and Oakland. For thrill-starved Steeler fanatics, this string was tantamount to the Pittsburgh Pirates' having won the World Series in 1960. Bradshaw was pretty excited, too.

"I was on cloud nine," he says. "Everything was great. I felt like I owed everybody something because I had been a first draft choice and because Pittsburgh had always been a losing team. I didn't care a lot about glory or anything like that. I just wanted to come in and win some football games."

The excitement, though, disappeared faster than hubcaps in the city's streets. There was less resemblance between the Steelers' pre-season and season than between *Mary Poppins* and *Deep Throat*.

Bradshaw's play in the early regular-season games was epitomized by his being tackled for safeties in each of the first three games. Furthermore, he didn't throw a touchdown pass until the fifth game and by the halfway point on the schedule, he was benched. For the season as a whole, the 6'3", 215-pound native of Shreveport, Louisiana, completed a miserably low 38 percent of his passes, had a league-high 24 tosses intercepted, was thrown for losses 25 times and finished 29th among the 31 passers who qualified for the official NFL standings. Only Boston's entry of Mike Taliaferro and Joe Kapp trailed him.

Before the season began, someone had asked Len Dawson, a veteran of 13 pro seasons, what advice he would give to a youngster like Bradshaw, who was entering a situation much the same as Dawson had in 1957 as No. 1 draft choice with Pittsburgh.

"He should go in," Dawson said, "with the idea that he doesn't know it all, that he's going to have to work, that he has things to learn before he can tell the team anything with confidence. And it's tough. The only way to get that confidence is through experience. I'd say that good advice to Bradshaw or any other young quarterback is basically to keep your mouth shut, do the best job you possibly can and to work at it. Don't worry about making comments."

It's doubtful whether Bradshaw ever heard that advice. He should have.

For one thing, Bradshaw felt he could learn everything there was to learn in one year. For another, he didn't exactly keep his mouth shut. That was probably his biggest mistake and it happened after he was removed from the Cincinnati game in favor of Hanratty.

Bradshaw, a garrulous person who always speaks candidly and seldom hides his feelings, couldn't keep his disappointment to himself that day. He was crushed and humiliated and he told the world about it.

"I don't want to play second fiddle to Hanratty," he told writers, standing only a couple of feet from Hanratty. "I don't mind playing behind somebody older, someone ready to retire, but I surely won't play behind someone my age. If the Steelers are going to do that, they better trade me."

The outburst came within a week after the young quarterback first came late to a team meeting and then missed a practice (he had gone home after a game in Houston and his plane to Pittsburgh was canceled), and the combination was too much for Coach Chuck Noll. "Terry has a lot of growing up to do," Noll said, "both on the field and off it."

Bradshaw began maturing off the field between seasons and on the field once the next season arrived.

"By the time the [first] season ended," he says, "I just wanted to get away from Pittsburgh. All I wanted was to go home. I wanted to relax and get football out of my mind. At that time, I didn't know if I ever wanted to play again."

Once he was home in Louisiana, though, Terry had calmed down enough to be able to start thinking about what had happened and what had to happen for him to fulfill the promise with which he had come to the NFL.

"I learned a lot in the six months I was away; I learned a lot without even touching a football," he says. "I learned I had to grow up, both on the field and off. I decided there had to be a lot of studying and a lot of adjustments to be made and a lot of pressures to overcome. In that first season, I started losing my confidence and when that happened, I started pressing."

When he returned to the Steelers after undergoing his mental metamorphosis, Bradshaw found the man who would help him change some of his bad ways as a quarterback, too. Aware that they had a diamond that needed some expert polishing, the Steelers hired Babe Parilli, a veteran pro quarterback, as quarterback coach. Parilli did for Bradshaw what Madison Avenue did for Richard Nixon: he converted him from a failure into a success.

"Babe talks my language and I talk his," Bradshaw said after working with Parilli for only a few months. "I can tell him anything on my mind and he understands it and he'll react. I think of him as a big brother who knows an awful lot about football. The big thing he does is not letting me get down. He keeps me up. I'm my own worst critic, but Babe doesn't let me get down on myself."

As far as the physical part of the game is concerned, Parilli taught Bradshaw not to rifle his passes as hard as he could. Too many times in his rookie year his passes bounced off his receivers and into the waiting hands of the defense. Parilli showed Terry how he could still get his passes to his receivers in a hurry but in a way that made them more catchable.

The results of the reeducation of Terry Bradshaw were glaring: from a completion percentage of 38 he soared to 54; from an interception of 11 he dropped to 6 (and 4 in 1972); from 6 touchdown passes he improved to 13.

"Joe Namath is a great quarterback and Terry Bradshaw is going to be a great quarterback," said Parilli, who played behind Namath for two years with the New York Jets. "I don't think Namath can set up to pass any quicker than Terry, and Bradshaw's arm is as good as anyone's anywhere."

No one ever questioned Bradshaw's arm. Many quarterbacks watch in awe as he heaves a football downfield as easily as if his right arm had a bazooka opening at the end. He always had the arm, even in high school, when he set a national record by throwing the javelin 244 feet, 11 inches. But for the arm to be effective in professional football, the mind has to be strong, too.

"It starts when you drop back," Bradshaw says. "You've got to keep your poise, keep your cool. I didn't do that my first year. Everything I did was in a rush, hurrying my passes, forcing my handoffs, quick with my fakes. Now I try to have a good time, relax and enjoy it. I try to sit in the pocket and act cool. When you do this and read your keys, you're going to do all right. When I stay in there with my poise, I can read defenses. I read them real well as long as I stand in there long enough to look at them."

When it's necessary, Bradshaw isn't afraid to run with the ball. He's one of the young crop of big, strong quarterbacks and can be as tough to bring down sometimes as a running back. It's only when he is hit as hard and falls as he did against the Dolphins in the conference championship game that the Steelers worry. Still, the Steelers scored on the play (Gerry Mullins, a guard, recovered Bradshaw's fumble in the end zone for the touchdown) and in the closing minutes of the game had a chance to end Miami's perfect season. In his desperation to try and pull it out, though, Bradshaw completed two passes to Dolphin defenders in the final three minutes.

"I felt confident we could do it, but I threw bad passes," Bradshaw said in his usual candor. "I intended to lob the ball both times, but when I threw it, it went straight."

Despite occasional errant plays, though, the Steelers have gone straight toward the top with Bradshaw, which is higher than they ever went with Unitas, Dawson, Layne, Morall and Nelsen.

John Brodie

As Y. A. Tittle limped off the field, a pulled leg muscle ending his afternoon on this Sunday in December, the San Francisco 49ers saw their title hopes limping with him. Here they were, losing to the Baltimore Colts 13–10 but on the Colts' 15-yard line with less than a minute remaining in the next-to-last game of the season.

Surely, Tittle, the old pro, the wily veteran, would have been able to get them into the end zone and keep those title chances breathing, but now the new kid, John Brodie, was in Tittle's spot and it wasn't an envious one. Brodie, a rookie from Stanford, had played less than ten minutes in the first ten games and had thrown only seven passes. Now he was experiencing his first pressure situation and when he stepped into the huddle, he laughed.

"What are you laughing about?" asked Hugh McElhenny, the 49ers' outstanding runner, who saw nothing very funny about the situation.

"This is a funny way to get started," the bewildered youngster replied. But it wasn't funny when he couldn't decide what play to call.

Finally, Brodie selected a pass to Billy Wilson, but the toss into the end zone missed. Then McElhenny returned to the huddle and suggested "47X", a pass to McElhenny in the left flat. Having no better idea for the fourth-down, seconds-left play, Brodie accepted the suggestion, then dropped back and looped a pass over the head of Milt Davis, the Colts' all-pro cornerback. McElhenny caught it and the 49ers won, 17–13.

"Brodie's timing was perfect," McElhenny said later. "Another second and it would have been too late."

"A rookie couldn't have faced a more clutch situation," said Frankie Albert, the 49ers' head coach.

The calendar now speeds ahead fifteen years, and the 49ers again are in a clutch situation. This time they're playing the Minnesota Vikings in the last game of the season and again the division title is at stake. The 49ers didn't win that title in 1957 (they lost a playoff to Detroit) and it didn't appear that they would win this one either. A little more than a quarter remained, but they were losing 17–6 and they hadn't shown much life all day.

Steve Spurrier was the 49er quarterback this day, just as he had been the previous eight games while Brodie recuperated from a severely sprained ankle. But now, with 1½ minutes left in the third quarter, Coach Dick Nolan sent Brodie in to replace Spurrier, hoping somehow the old pro, the wily veteran could instill some spark into a lethargic, inept offense.

At first Brodie had trouble readjusting to the game situation, and Viking defenders picked off two of his passes just as they had stolen three of Spurrier's. But the next time San Francisco got the ball—on its own one-yard line, of all places—Brodie was ready to roll.

He passed to John Isenbarger for 12 yards, then connected with the brilliant Gene Washington for 53 yards. An 8-yarder to Vic Wash-

ington followed, and the drive ended when Gene Washington grabbed a 24-yard pass for a touchdown. Just like that the 49ers had reduced their deficit to 17–13 and there was still time, six minutes of time, for them to turn that deficit into an advantage.

The only problem was the Vikings, directed by the resourceful Fran Tarkenton, consumed 4½ minutes of those six minutes, and the 49ers were left with little time when they got the ball back at their 34-yard line.

Brodie's first play was a pass to Larry Schreiber for 9 yards and his second was an 8-yarder to Vic Washington. He missed Ted Kwalick on his third toss, but pass interference gave San Francisco the ball at the Minnesota 26. Two plays later, Brodie found Vic Washington on the left side for an 18-yard gain to the 2.

"I hadn't played in so long there were only a few plays I could call," Brodie said later. "The fancy stuff was out. I decided to try three passes and then run as a last resort."

Two of the passes didn't work. With twenty-five seconds left, though, Brodie tried the third and this one sped into Dick Witcher's arms in the end zone for the reserve receiver's first touchdown of the season, a 20–17 victory and the Western Division title of the National Conference.

"It was a hell of a game, the one I wanted most to win," said Brodie who in his first game in two months completed 10 of 15 passes.

These two clutch situations occurred fifteen years apart, perhaps even in different lifetimes as far as Brodie and his pro status were concerned. But they tell a lot about the man who has quarterbacked one team longer than any other quarterback in the game today. He has survived three coaches (Nolan is the fourth he's served) and he has watched the NFL grow from twelve teams to twenty-six. He has thrown for more than 30,000 yards, a feat achieved by only two other quarterbacks (John Unitas and Y. A. Tittle), and he has completed a healthy 55 percent of his passes.

He's also heard a lot of derisive comments from the 49er fans, but that seems to be as much a part of the game as the flask for fans who take out their displeasure of a team's failure on the quarterback.

"I've never tried to figure out the fans," Brodie says. "Rather than look for reasons for their booing, I go out and play my game. I have no feeling of animosity toward the fans."

The San Francisco fans were particularly frustrated in the first thirteen years of Brodie's career because, like the outstanding quarterbacks before him (Frankie Albert and Y. A. Tittle, for example), he didn't have enough talent with him that would take the 49ers to a championship. Then came 1970.

In the team's first game that season, Brodie completed 17 of 20 passes in powering the 49ers past the Washington Redskins, 26–17, and they built from there. Unlike the wind that blows in the Bay area, though, winning their first division title was not a breeze for the 49ers. In fact, after they lost to their arch rivals, the Los Angeles Rams, 30–13, they had to win their final three games or have their season end like all the others.

With Brodie leading the way, that's exactly what the 49ers did. They won the games, coming from behind in each. In the three contests, Brodie passed for 647 yards and 7 touchdowns while having only 1 toss intercepted. His performance enabled the 49ers to finish with a 10-3-1 record—their best since moving into the NFL from the defunct All-America Conference —and to advance to the playoffs against the Minnesota Vikings.

The prospect of playing the Vikings, first of all, and in Minnesota, second of all, couldn't have been very enticing to the 49ers, but after all the years they had waited they weren't about to run away from the team with the league's best record and a temperature that was eight degrees above zero at game time.

"When we were working on the game plan for the Vikings," Brodie recalls, "I talked to our defense and they said they didn't think Minnesota would score much on us. There are certain teams which our defense thinks we stack up well against, and every time they told me they could stop another team, they were right. They told me they could hold the Vikings so I decided we wouldn't have to take many chances during the game. As it worked out, they were right."

Brodie threw 32 passes at the Vikings, hitting on half of them for 201 yards. One of the 16 completions went for a touchdown and the quarterback ran for another score as the 49ers won, 17–14.

Their good fortune, though, didn't hold for another week, and they lost in their final bid to make the Super Bowl, dropping a 17–10 decision to the Dallas Cowboys.

Nevertheless, Brodie led the league in pass completions, yards gained and touchdown passes, and he was considered to be the prime factor in San Francisco's success. As such, he was named the league's Most Valuable Player.

Until that moment, John Brodie had been best known as a player who profited most from the merger between the NFL and the AFL in 1966. He profited to the amount of $750,000, the price the AFL Houston Oilers offered Brodie to leave the NFL 49ers and sign a five-year contract with them.

Don Klosterman wrote the figure on a piece of paper, but it never got as far as a contract because the leagues reached agreement on a merger. However, when Brodie heard the news, he said, "Somebody owes me $750,000." And to make sure he collected, Brodie hired an attorney, John Elliott Cook, who as a specialist in corporate and business law was familiar with large sums of money.

At Cook's suggestion, Brodie took his family to Hawaii instead of reporting to the 49er camp in July, 1967, while negotiations were going on. Being in camp, the attorney reasoned, would weaken the quarterback's bargaining position. In the end, Brodie himself weakened but not by much. Admitting he was anxious to start playing football, Brodie signed for the $750,000 package, whereas if he had waited a little longer he probably could have received closer to $1 million. Since both leagues were involved in the situation—the merger was the crux of the argument—all teams wound up paying a share of Brodie's booty.

It was certainly far more than Brodie ever could have earned playing golf, a possibility he considered earlier in his football career. When Brodie, a native of San Francisco, went to Stanford, he had intended playing baseball and basketball but he wound up playing football and golf. When the 49ers made him their first-round draft pick in 1957, he continued his interest in football, but he never lost his desire for golf. That's why he spent two springs and two winters on the pro golf tour early in his football career.

"My wife and I and our daughter, who at that time was a baby, were traveling around on the tour, living in a different motel each week," Brodie recalls. "It was tough. Besides, trying to have two careers in sports was rapidly becoming impossible. I finally had to make a choice, and I thought my best shot was in football."

Brodie shoots in the low 70s, but according to his wife, Sue, "In his mind, he must be tops in anything he attempts or it's not worth the effort. He found he'd never be anywhere near that in golf so he decided just to play the game for the fun of it. But he had to try."

There were times, though, that Brodie had to wonder if the 49ers considered him tops at quarterback. They kept bringing in people like Bill Kilmer and George Mira and Steve Spurrier as if they were hoping someone could beat him out for the No. 1 job. That's why Brodie went

to Dick Nolan when he became the head coach in 1968 and asked him about his quarterback plans. Brodie had heard he was ripe for trading and that one of the younger quarterbacks, Mira or Spurrier, would replace him.

"The best man will get the job," Nolan told him. "If you're the best, you'll get it."

Given that kind of straightforward thinking, Brodie went out and proved he was the best. He retained his job and proceeded to have one of his best years, completing 58 percent of his passes for 3,020 yards and 22 touchdowns. After a slight dip in production the following season, he led the 49ers to three consecutive division championships, including the one in 1972, when he came off the bench and rallied the team past the Vikings with two long touchdown drives in the final quarter.

It was a fitting turn in the career of the man who grew up in the area that also produced such professional athletes as Frank Robinson, Curt Flood, Vada Pinson and Bill Russell, and it helped turn off the fan abuse that had been heaped on Brodie's head (the beer cans as well as the derogatory words).

"I don't know how the fans feel," said Paul Wiggin, 49ers' assistant coach and formerly defensive end with Cleveland, "but when I was in Cleveland, we knew you couldn't get to John Brodie. He doesn't panic. There are quarterbacks in the league who can be pressured, but John Brodie isn't one of them. We'd much rather have seen Mira starting against us than Brodie. You'd try to psyche out John, yelling stuff across the line, and he'd give it right back to you. I've never been more impressed with any quarterback."

And he wasn't talking about Brodie's bankroll.

Len Dawson

Len Dawson is one of the few professional football players who played long enough to qualify for pensions in both the National and the American Leagues before they merged. There were times, though, when he didn't think he could qualify for a free pass into any ballpark.

Dawson was a heralded quarterback from Purdue who was a first-round draft choice of the Pittsburgh Steelers in 1957. As such, he was expected to become a star in the NFL before too many autumns breezed by. But Johnny Carson never would have become much of a television celebrity if he had sat behind the camera while Jack Paar and Steve Allen worked in front of it.

This, in effect, is what happened to Dawson. For three years in Pittsburgh he sat on the bench while Bobby Layne quarterbacked the Steelers; for two more years he watched Milt Plum handle the job in Cleveland. Heralded players who fall into that syndrome have a habit of rapidly fading into obscurity and a pit of self-doubt.

"After a while," Dawson says, "I had serious doubts of my ability. In five years in the NFL, I started two games, including preseason games. I never played two games in a row. I never started and finished a game. I had to ask myself why. One conclusion was that I wasn't good enough."

At Purdue, Dawson completed 54 percent of his 452 passes and averaged better than 1 touchdown pass a game. In his first five years as a pro, however, he threw only 45 passes and completed 21. Only 2 of those completions went for touchdowns.

As Dawson played less and less (he appeared in only eight games for the Browns in two years), Hank Stram watched, from a distance, with great puzzlement. After all, Stram had helped recruit Dawson for Purdue out of Alliance, Ohio, and he was one of the coaches closest to Lenny in his first three years at the Big-Ten school. Now, while he tried to get the young Dallas Texans of the young AFL off the ground, Stram couldn't understand why his former student wasn't playing more in the other league.

Finally, one winter Stram was in Pittsburgh for a convention and he saw Dawson. "He was very dejected," Stram recalls. "I tried to assure him that he still could play, that probably all he needed was a different atmosphere. I told him I'd like to have him with our team if he ever got free."

Dawson couldn't have been more determined to get his release from the Browns than if he had been a slave in the pre-Civil War days who was told a million dollars awaited him if he could win his freedom. After the 1961 season, Dawson went to Paul Brown, the Cleveland coach, explained his feelings to him and expressed a strong desire to play for Stram.

Brown, who usually is pictured as a hard-bitten, unfeeling machine, promptly displayed the compassionate side of him that most people never see: he placed Dawson on waivers and it wasn't long before the young, but growing-old quarterback was a Texan.

As soon as the Dallas camp opened, though, it instantly became obvious to Stram that this wasn't the same Dawson he remembered.

"Len had developed a lot of bad habits while he was inactive," Stram expains. "He was slow, sloppy getting under the center and taking the snap and carrying the ball too low, dropping back into the pocket. Then when he did throw, I noticed he was winding up. He had his work cut out, but I was patient with him. I knew he was a dedicated athlete and by working hard he could put it all back together again."

As is obvious from his record since then, Dawson indeed put it back together. He established a flock of AFL records, including the mark for completion percentage (61) in his first year in the league, and he led the team to two Super Bowls, being named most valuable player in the second when the Kansas City Chiefs (originally Dallas Texans) defeated the Minnesota Vikings for the championship.

Dawson is the first to admit that he never could have done it without Stram. It's most likely that any other coach, seeing what Stram saw in that 1962 camp, would have released Dawson without even writing his name down on the team's depth chart. Since that time, though, Stram and Dawson have formed a relationship that seldom has existed between a coach and his quarterback in the more than fifty years the pro game has been played. In fact, there isn't another quarterback playing today who has served under the same coach for as long as Dawson and Stram have been together.

The coach and the quarterback have been through a lot in a dozen years, but nothing has been as trying as the events of the 1969 season. The season began with a serious physical ailment and ended with excruciating mental anguish. Overcoming it all, though, Dawson emerged with his greatest success.

The physically damaging aspect of the season developed on a September Sunday afternoon in Boston, during the Chiefs' 31–0 route of the Patriots. Although it wasn't too noticeable at the time, Dawson suffered an injury to his left knee that threatened to end his year right then and there. The Chiefs, though, wanted to explore every possible avenue before conceding the season.

Dawson visited two of the country's leading orthopedic surgeons to get their opinion of what would have to be done. The first said to operate and was ready to do so at that moment. But Dawson wanted to see the other orthopedist before making his decision. The second one suggested that the problem, a mild ligament tear, might heal by itself if Dawson rested the knee for five or six weeks. Although the choices were clear-cut—operate and forget the rest of the season, don't operate and maybe play toward the end—the decision was not.

"I wanted to play," Dawson says. "I had never been out before except for a game or two and I couldn't really believe the injury was that serious. I had worked awfully hard this year and things were going well. If I laid out for the season, I'd be a thirty-five-year-old quarterback with a knee operation and that's not a very good position to be in. But in the end I guess my strongest motivation was the possibility of us winning the league championship and going to the Super Bowl. It would have been one thing if I was on a team that didn't have a chance, but I was on a team that had a real shot."

And so, Dawson passed up the operation and waited. For six weeks he waited. Finally, when his substitute, rookie Mike Livingston, seemed to have run out of victories, he returned to the lineup and led the Chiefs the rest of the way to the Super Bowl.

Super Bowl IV. The game really didn't have Roman numerals then, but if you have a Super Bowl VII, somewhere along the line there had to be a Super Bowl IV. For the Chiefs, there also was a Super Bowl I. It was against the Green Bay Packers, of course, and only the most zealous AFL patriots (with a small p) gave the Chiefs a chance.

The teams played evenly in the first half with the Packers taking a 14–10 lead at half time, but early in the third quarter Willie Wood intercepted a Dawson pass and ignited a 35–10 romp for the NFL champions.

Three years later, Dawson finally had received his fondest wish—to get back to the Super Bowl—and he was going to atone for that intercepted pass by leading the Chiefs past the Minnesota Vikings. Early in the week prior to the game, though, Dawson learned that atonement wasn't going to be that easy. The Vikings, of course, represented a difficult enough roadblock for Dawson, especially with their fierce front four. But an unexpected roadblock landed directly on Dawson's 6′, 190-pound frame.

A television report out of Detroit the Tuesday evening before the game told of a grand jury investigation of sports gambling. Names of several football players were mentioned in connection with the investigation. One of those names was Len Dawson.

The Chiefs were stunned, although no one so deeply as Dawson himself. He had no idea what it was all about, but he knew it wasn't good. Finally, he learned that his name had been linked with that of Donald Dawson, no relative but a man he met about ten years before and with whom he had only a casual acquaintance.

If such a report had come in the middle of the summer, it would have been bad enough. But here it was Super Bowl week and the eyes of the country were focused on New Orleans. Everyone wanted to know what Len Dawson had to say about Don Dawson, and they heard, when the quarterback read a statement to a press conference late that first evening.

Although that statement finished Dawson's public discussion of the situation, he couldn't dismiss it from his mind entirely (nor could he dismiss the abuse his family was taking in Kansas City). The investigation and whatever remote role he might have in it preyed on his mind the rest of the week and made it difficult for him to think about the Vikings, a team that required a great deal of thought.

Nevertheless, when Sunday arrived, Dawson was chanting signals as if nothing had happened. He called plays and handed off and passed (12 for 17) the same way, and the result was a 23–7 upset of the vexed Vikings. Probably no player in the history of athletics ever had to play such an important game under such pressure. If the Chiefs had lost, suspicious critics would have pointed to various moves by Dawson as proof that he had played less than his best for what they would have said were obvious reasons. They never got the chance.

With such a tremendous personal, as well as team, victory in his grasp, Dawson easily could have retired after that game, a move that would have made his wife, Jackie, extremely happy. She had been after him to retire for several years. But Dawson had no thought of retiring. In fact, it wasn't until after the 1971 season and a frustrating overtime loss to Miami in the playoffs that he even considered such a move.

As with his knee injury in 1969, this decision was a difficult one. He would be thirty-seven years old before the next season started and he had played fifteen years.

"Had someone told me fifteen years ago that I would play fifteen years of pro football, I would have told them they were crazy," Dawson said.

But he had played fifteen years and he wasn't ready to stop at that. Nor was Stram about to encourage him to stop. "I think it's a mistake for a player to retire," the coach said, "when he (1) still has the will to play and (2) is physically capable of expressing that will to play. Len has always been a great competitor and truly loves the game."

The decision, however, wasn't Stram's. Nor was it Dawson's teammates', even though Ed Podolak had conveyed what undoubtedly was the team's collective feeling when he approached the quarterback after the sudden death loss to the Dolphins and said, "Lennie, you can't quit playing now, not after a game like this."

But the coach and the team were factors Dawson considered before making his decision. So was the Pro Bowl a month after the Miami letdown. In that game, Dawson took over at quarterback for the American Conference All-Stars in the second half and directed his team to a 26–12 victory. "The success I had in the Pro Bowl," he said, "proved that my problems weren't serious. "I was playing among the very best players in my profession and to do as well as I did was a gratifying thing."

Finally, Dawson considered conversations he had had with players who had retired not too long before. "They all told me they would have played on if they could have physically," Dawson related. "I didn't have any serious injury in 1971. Every professional player realizes that the day will come when he must retire. Were I to retire before I'm ready, I would have to live with that the rest of my life and I'm not ready to do that."

When Dawson does retire, he'll leave behind a record of passing accuracy that has few parallels. He led the AFL in completion percentage six times, he once completed 15 straight passes in a game and he has completed 56.3 percent of all the passes he has thrown in sixteen seasons.

Yet, no one ever hears Dawson telling people how good he is. "I'm not outspoken," he says. "I don't come out to do any bragging. I don't like to draw attention to myself."

His record does that well enough.

Bob Griese

A poet once wrote that the saddest words are "it might have been." For the Pittsburgh Steelers, though, the saddest words are these: "Are you ready?" "Yeah."

There's nothing special about the words—except when they're spoken (1) by Don Shula and Bob Griese and (2) during a Miami game with the Steelers. The combination has occurred twice, and twice it's been fatal to the Steelers. The first time, in 1971, the words helped keep the Steelers from winning their first title of any kind. The second time, in 1972, they prevented the Steelers from winning a conference championship for the first time after they had won their first title of any kind.

On the evening before the first instance, Griese was rushed to the hospital with a stomach ailment. He was in uniform the next day when the game began, but he was too weak to play so George Mira started. "The way I felt Saturday night," Griese said, "I never felt I'd put on a uniform against the Steelers, much less play."

But the Steelers jumped to a 14–3 lead, and Shula began to get a little nervous. He walked over to Griese and looked at his pale quarterback.

"Are you ready?"

"Yeah."

Griese fumbled the ball on his first play, and the Steelers recovered and proceeded to score another touchdown, increasing their lead to 21–3. But the Dolphin quarterback came back and fired a 12-yard touchdown pass to Paul Warfield. Then he combined with Warfield on an 86-yard touchdown pass. Finally he hit Warfield with a 60-yarder and Miami won, 24–21.

About thirteen months later the teams were playing again, this time for the American Conference championship. This time Earl Morrall started for Miami at quarterback because he had started the previous ten games while Griese was recovering from a broken leg and a dislocated ankle. By half time, however, the Dolphins' attack was sputtering and with the game tied, 7–7, Shula walked up to Griese in the locker room.

"Are you ready?"

"Yeah."

The Steelers took a 10–7 lead in the early minutes of the third quarter and then Griese entered the game. Choosing his plays carefully, he directed the Dolphins on an 11-play, 80-yard drive that consumed half the quarter and culminated in Jim Kiick's 2-yard touchdown burst around right end and a 14–10 lead.

Two series later, early in the fourth quarter, Griese took the Dolphins on another 11-play drive, this one covering 49 yards in six minutes and ending with Kiick smashing over left tackle for the touchdown that turned out to be the decisive score in the 21–17 affair.

By that time, the Steelers were ready, too—ready to pick up Griese and gently drop him into the watery spot near Three Rivers Stadium where the Allegheny and the Monongahela rivers meet to form the Ohio.

In recent seasons, though, more and more NFL teams have acquired that kind of feeling about Griese. Belittled in his early pro years as too small and weak-armed, the 6'1", 190-pound Dolphin has emerged as one of the outstanding quarterbacks in the game today. He is, of course, surrounded by the strongest supporting cast in the NFL, but that doesn't detract from the qualities he has exhibited, particularly since Don Shula became the Miami coach in 1970, Griese's fourth year in the league.

"He's got so much confidence in himself that we have total confidence in him," says Larry Csonka. "He's done it for us before. In the championship game with Pittsburgh, you could just feel us start to lift."

"He's got a mind like a saber slash," Nick Buoniconti says. "He looks at a defense and he knows exactly how he wants to pick it apart. I've seen him come an awful long way in four years. Now he is imperturbable. He never shows panic or upset. Never. Once there was a lot of talk that Griese would never make it in this league. They used to say he was worried about getting hurt. Now you could jam it down his throat and he would still make the play. All of us know that he will sooner or later. We know it's just a matter of time and then he'll do it for us."

One of the things Griese does especially well for Miami is call the right play at the right time. John Unitas always has been considered a master at shrewdly selecting the right plays; it's possible Griese is replacing him as the reigning master in that area.

"He makes their team," says Norm Bulaich, a former teammate of Unitas's. "He's a great play caller."

Perhaps the ultimate in Griese's play calling came in the longest game ever played, the sudden death playoff game between Miami and

Kansas City in 1971. The Dolphins had the ball in the sixth quarter at their 35 with second down and 5 yards needed for a first down, and the quarterback called for a roll-right trap.

"I'd have to say that that was probably the best play Bob called all year," says Norm Evans, the tackle who is an original Dolphin.

The Chiefs had been pretty successful all day in stopping Miami's sweeps, but on this play the flow started out to the right, like a sweep, only to have Larry Csonka take a handoff from Griese and run to the left. The Chiefs went for the fake completely and Csonka wound up running for 29 yards and setting up Garo Yepremian's winning field goal.

The following week, in the conference title game against Baltimore, Griese noticed that the Colt defense was bunching up to stop Csonka so he called a play-action pass that began with a fake to Csonka that froze the defensive backs but wound up as a 75-yard scoring pass to Paul Warfield.

Some critics suggest Griese's job is made simple by the presence of such fine running backs as Csonka, Kiick and Mercury Morris. All he has to do, they say, is hand the ball to one of them and step out of the way. It isn't that simple, of course. No matter how good his backs are, a quarterback must have a feeling for which play to call when.

"Passing is about 50 percent of my job," says Griese, who was one of a long line of top-notch quarterbacks produced by Purdue. "The other 50 percent is play calling. I study as much on the running game as I do on the passing game. A quarterback had better have an understanding of the passing game, but he also has to understand the running game. When to call it is the thing."

Where to go to college was the thing for Griese in 1963, after a star-studded multi-sports high school career in Evansville, Indiana. He wanted to go to Notre Dame, but the Irish recruiters apparently decided he was too small. So he wound up at Purdue where as a junior, he led the Boilermakers to a 25–21 upset of the No. 1-ranked Irish by completing 19 of 22 passes.

While making a name for himself as a top college quarterback, Griese still wasn't as highly thought of as Steve Spurrier, the Heisman Trophy winner. The Dolphins, who were only one year old, would have grabbed Spurrier in the draft if he had been available—after all, he was a native of Miami Beach—but he went to San Francisco, so Miami had to settle for Griese. That, of course, is like saying that Carlo Ponti, the Italian movie magnate, had to settle for Sophia Loren as his wife.

Although John Stofa was the No. 1 quarterback when Griese arrived in Miami, the rookie wasn't No. 2 long enough to try harder. Stofa broke an ankle in the early minutes of Miami's first game against Denver in 1967, and Griese made an unexpected debut. He was an instant hit, completing 12 of 19 passes for 193 yards and 2 touchdowns as Miami won, 35–21. Later on that season, he established an American League record by completing 81 percent of his tosses, 17 out of 21, against the New York Jets. Still later, he set another mark by throwing 122 consecutive passes without an interception.

Generally, however, Griese's career proceeded in a less than spectacular fashion. In fact, at the midway mark of the 1970 season, it looked as if he had become a spectacular flop. After the Dolphins had won four of the first five games that year, they suddenly turned around and dropped successive decisions to Cleveland, Baltimore and Philadelphia as Griese had 8 passes intercepted, giving him a total of 14 for the season.

A growing segment of the Miami following wanted Shula to bench Griese, but on the plane trip home from Philadelphia, the coach told Griese he would remain in the lineup. "I didn't think those losses were entirely his fault," Shula explained. "He had played poorly in spots, but there also were dropped passes and killing penalties. That was as much of a factor in the slump as Griese."

In the next game, against New Orleans, Griese responded to Shula's confidence in him by hitting on 15 of 19 passes as the Dolphins started a six-game winning streak that would take them to the playoffs for the first time.

After that, of course, the Dolphins didn't simply make the playoffs. They went to the Super Bowl the next two years and threatened to be a participant for many years to come.

In spite of the Dolphins' sizzling success, though, Griese plummeted to one of the lowest points of his career in 1972, when he suffered a dislocated ankle and a broken bone just above the ankle in a game against San Diego and had to watch from the sidelines as Earl Morrall directed his team to an unbeaten season.

Griese emerged with the double injury from an unscheduled meeting with two large members of San Diego's front four. Deacon Jones, 6′ 5″,

250 pounds, hit Griese high, and Ron East, 6′4″, 245, hit him low.

"You have to go after a guy as good as he is when he's scrambling," a disturbed Jones said afterward. "But I don't like to see anybody hurt like that. We need people like him in the NFL. I'm sorry he's hurt that bad—really, really sorry."

"I knew something was wrong as soon as it happened," said Griese, who was injured after throwing a pass. "I felt like I knew I wasn't going to be in there for the next play. My main concern was how long I would be out—one or two or how many games."

Griese was out until the final game of the season, when he played only briefly as a tuneup for the playoffs. The time dragged by slowly, and it was a time of great frustration for him.

"The day you hurt the ankle you know it's going to be a difficult period of time," Griese said. "It's a disturbing thing, not practicing or playing with the team. But my only attitude was a positive one. I was going to do everything I could to get the leg well."

The leg was better by the end of the season and it felt particularly good in the championship game against Pittsburgh. His arm was good, too, and that's why Shula decided to start him in place of Morrall in the Super Bowl against Washington.

"Griese has come along real well from the ankle injury," the coach said in disclosing his plans. "I feel the strongest possible way we can go into the game is with Griese at quarterback."

As usual, Shula was right. Griese completed 8 of 11 passes, including all 6 he tried in the first half, as the Dolphins won the NFL championship, 14–7.

"I was ready to play," Griese said. "I told everybody that during the week. Somebody said that a lot of people didn't think I was ready. I didn't go out to prove to anybody but the ballplayers that we could win the game. It was a very satisfying time for me. I was very depressed when I got hurt. I didn't know if my season was over or not. I decided I was just going to try to work as hard as I could to recover and if there was any season left, I'd be ready."

And he was, just like he was against the Steelers.

John Hadl

It was such a pleasant spring day in the San Diego area that Charneil and John Hadl decided to go horseback riding. It wasn't one of the better plays Hadl had called in his nine years as a pro quarterback. Horses, Hadl learned, can be more dangerous than a whole line of Bubba Smiths and Alan Pages.

"I usually ride three or four times a year, but you wouldn't consider me a horseman," Hadl explained. "My horse was going full speed when the saddle started slipping. We came to a ditch with a tree across it. That's all I remember until I woke up in the hospital the next day."

Jackie DeLong, wife of Steve DeLong, a San Diego Charger defensive lineman, remembers what happened in between.

"It was the most horrible thing I've ever seen," said Mrs. DeLong, who was riding with the Hadls on that day in 1971. "We were returning to the stables and were riding full gallop along the trail. The saddle slipped from John's mount and caused him to fall. There was a large dead tree right in the middle of the trail. It's been there forever.

"The horses have been over that trail numerous times. I know they step over an object like that, but John fell just as his horse reached the tree. John struck the left side of his head on the tree and the blood just poured out. It was a horrible sight. I was riding so close behind him I thought my horse would trample him. After he struck the tree there was blood coming from his eye and ears. I don't think anyone who isn't as tough physically as John is could have take a blow like that."

Charneil Hadl was riding further behind her husband and didn't see what happened. "All I could see was a cloud of dust," she said. "When I reached him, he had blood all over his face. He couldn't breathe. It was just terrible."

An ambulance arrived about twenty minutes after the mishap and rushed Hadl to a hospital, where he underwent surgery for damage to his left eye. He suffered a fracture of the floor orbit of the eye, as well as a fractured skull, facial injuries and a severely bruised knee.

"I didn't realize how serious I'd been hurt until three or four days after the accident," he said.

The seriousness of the eye injury was explained by Dr. Paul Woodward, the Chargers' team physician.

"His vision wasn't impaired," Dr. Woodward said. "He could still see out of the eye, but he couldn't move it to look up, down or sideways. There are four muscles in the eye. It's like a team of four horses (not a particularly pleasant analogy for Hadl at the time). If one pulls in one direction, it's impossible for the others to move in another. The floor orbit fracture trapped the eye muscles and they couldn't function until it was repaired."

Hadl, of course, couldn't have played football until it was repaired either; the job is tough enough for a quarterback who can see all parts of the field, let alone for one who can look only straight ahead. But within a month after the accident Hadl's vision was fine and he had no lingering headaches from the accident. It was a recovery typical of a man who never has missed a football game, in junior high and high school in Lawrence, Kansas, in college at the University of Kansas and in the AFL and NFL as one of the most prolific passers in the game.

In each of his last nine years with San Diego (he played for the Chargers for eleven seasons in all before being traded to the Los Angeles Rams following the 1972 season), Hadl threw for more than 2,000 yards, three times exceeding the 3,000 mark.

Early in his final season with the Chargers, the balding quarterback became the ninth player in pro football history to surpass the lofty level of 25,000 career yards. He joined a group that included John Unitas, John Brodie, Sonny Jurgensen, Fran Tarkenton, George Blanda, Norm Snead, Y. A. Tittle and Bobby Layne.

It was somewhere back in the first couple hundred yards that Hadl got the biggest break of his pro career. Playing in his second game as a pro, in 1962, Hadl threw a pass against the then New York Titans and tore the cartilage in some ribs. Only a few plays earlier, Jack Kemp fractured a finger when his hand struck a Titan helmet on the follow-through of a pass.

Faced with two injured quarterbacks, Coach Sid Gillman had to make a decision. After deliberating for a few days, Gillman decided to keep Hadl and waive Kemp. The Buffalo Bills claimed Kemp for $100, and even though the future U. S. Congressman was to lead the Bills to two American League championships, the move gave Hadl an opportunity to step up his pro training and experience.

Hadl would be the first to admit he needed all the training and experience he could get. He certainly didn't get much preparation for the pro game at Kansas, where he twice was named to All-America teams, but where he was a combination runner, passer and kicker.

"When I came into the pros, I really wasn't a quarterback," says the 6'1", 210-pound veteran. "At Kansas we used the Oklahoma split-T and if I threw ten times a game that was a lot. Usually the passes were sprint outs and came when we were ahead. I had to learn how to throw the football from the dropback and how to be a quarterback."

Hadl wanted to be a quarterback, and that's why he chose the Chargers, who drafted him in the third round, over the Detroit Lions of the NFL, who drafted him in the first.

"The Lions told me they'd make another Paul Hornung out of me," Hadl recalls. "But I knew I couldn't be another Hornung, not with my dazzling speed. At Kansas I was timed in 10.8 in the 100 and they accused me of jumping the gun. I wanted to be a quarterback because I figured I'd make more money, have more longevity and more responsibility."

The process of becoming a pro quarterback was long and arduous and required many hours of extra work and study. "It took me three or four years to get the feel of throwing from the dropback and then I had to go through the learning process of how to be a field general," Hadl says. "That took another two years."

Because of his inexperience, Hadl sat on the bench through much of his second season while veteran Tobin Rote led the Chargers to the league championship. But from 1964 on, Hadl was the team's No. 1 quarterback and in several instances fought off spirited challenges to his job. He also became the team's unchallenged leader on the field.

"Men respond to a lot of intangibles," he says. "You've got to have the drive and purpose of a Bobby Layne. You've got to have a bushel of self-confidence. Take Namath. He knows what he can do and he does it and he sparks the team. You've got to wipe away all self-doubt. You've got to ignite people. You've got to lead."

Off the field, Hadl is as well-liked by players and friends as anyone. He's warm and friendly and he smiles a lot. But when he goes on the field, he leaves the warmth on the sideline and adopts the firmness necessary to run the team.

Once, running back Russ Smith strayed into an Oakland tackling contingent that resembled a meat grinder and he returned to the huddle bruised and bloody.

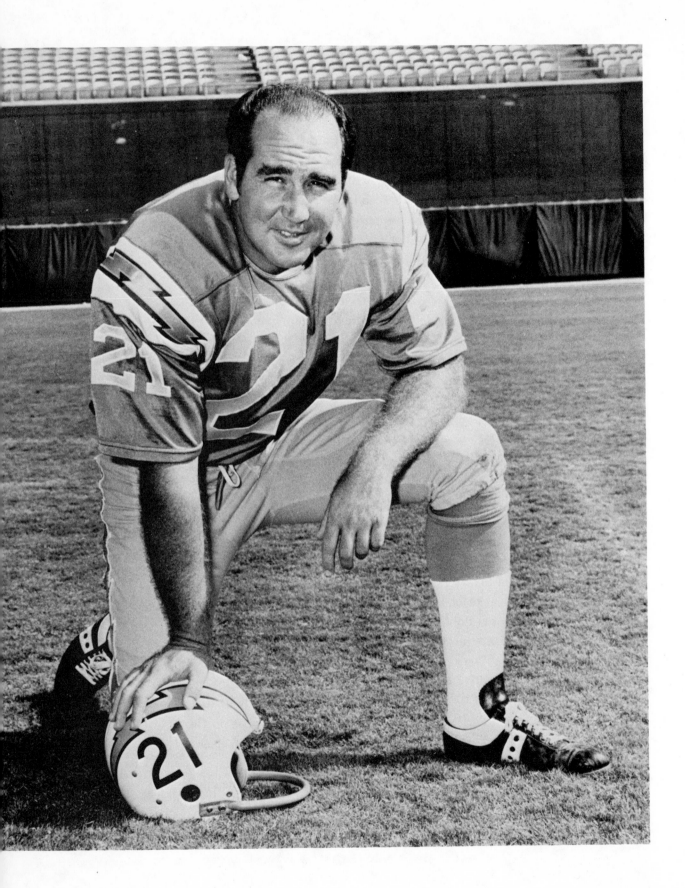

"There's blood coming out of your forehead, Russ," Hadl said. "Go back to the bench."

"I feel fine," Smith answered, putting his hand to his head as if to try and put a finger in the bleeding dike.

"Yeah," Hadl retorted, "but you're making me sick. Go to the bench." And Smith went to the bench.

That type of disagreement, though, is minor compared to some of the disputes Hadl has had with the people who commanded him—coach, general manager, owners. Most peculiar was the quarterback's relationship with Sid Gillman, long the general manager and coach of the Chargers. It seemed to be sort of a love-hate relationship with the love apparently as intense as the hate. Compounding the situation, though, was the occasional feud with the owners. Some of the fiery episodes stemmed from contract difficulties, others from playing status.

While Hadl was still relatively young, and after he had gone through a few years of education in Prof. Gillman's classes, he expressed his views on his teacher's ability.

"He undoubtedly has the finest mind in football," Hadl said of Gillman one summer day in 1965. "I can't conceive of another coach who can match his knowledge of the game or his dedication. Beyond that, he has the knack for expressing himself so that the players can grasp his ideas. Thanks to Sid, I'm getting a pretty good idea about the game. I've learned so much football under Gillman that I can give a lecture on it when I go home to Kansas after the season."

Less than two years later, though, Hadl was asking to be traded. "I've got to get away from that man," he said, meaning Gillman. "I can't stand another year. Basically, it's a personality clash. I feel the coach should show loyalty when the going gets tough."

When Gillman heard about Hadl's remarks, he said, "If that's the way he feels, he's gone. I'm not going to do anything to appease him."

Hadl was particularly upset that Gillman at times seemed to be looking for someone to beat him out for the No. 1 job.

"I had the distinct feeling one season [1966] he was trying to get rid of me when he started Steve Tensi in New York and Denver," Hadl commented. "He put Tensi in there hoping he'd win the job."

But three months after the bitter exchange of words, the two, like father and son, kissed and made up, and Hadl signed to play with the Chargers in 1967.

"John has become a great quarterback," the coach said. "Nobody in this game knows as much about it as he does. Nothing will ever develop in a game that will faze him."

But something fazed him because he played out his option in 1968; in other words, he didn't sign a contract for that season. He still hadn't signed as the free agent deadline, April 1, 1969, drew near. Instead he exchanged bitter words with Gene Klein, the club president, after Klein refused to give him a $250,000-loan for investment purposes.

"John is an excellent quarterback," the boss said, "but he's no Joe Namath by any stretch of the imagination."

"I may not be any Joe Namath, but Klein's no Sonny Werblin," Hadl retorted sharply, referring to the man who helped build the New York Jets by signing Namath.

Furthermore, the quarterback said, "I'm not considering signing with the Chargers. The way I feel now I'll be leaving San Diego. I don't know if anything can change my mind."

Something did, though, because Hadl signed again with the Chargers and stayed in San Diego until he had completed the 1972 season. Finally, after years of rumored trades and bitter and sweet words, the Chargers (Harland Svare by now was the general manager and coach) sent Hadl north to Los Angeles. Thus, for the second time in two years, the old dog had to learn new tricks, first the new system Svare installed at San Diego and then the Chuck Knox method with the Rams.

In leaving the American Conference, Hadl took with him a share of two AFL records—19 consecutive games in which he threw touchdown passes (overall at one point, he had tossed scoring passes in 35 of 36 games) and 6 passes intercepted in a game.

It was the latter problem that always disturbed Gillman. Hadl had a tendency to throw a lot of interceptions, especially in 1968 when he had 32 picked off. He drastically reduced that total to 26 in the following two seasons, but then his passes started taking off in the wrong direction again as 25 were grabbed by the opposition in 1971 and a league-high 26 in 1972. But Hadl always has remained undaunted by those errant tosses.

"If you're intercepted," he says, "it's either because you've thrown a lousy pass or the receiver has broken his pattern or your arm is pushed as you throw. Whatever happens wrong, the quarterback gets the blame. But that's what we get paid for—and we get paid the most."

Bill Kilmer

Bill Kilmer very possibly is the ultimate tribute to the talents that have made George Allen one of the most astute and successful coaches in the National Football League. Allen might not be the best liked coach in the league, but he can't be denied his record. And the line on that record that is perhaps more indicative than any victory of the ingredients of the man's whirring mind is the acquisition of Bill Kilmer.

On January 23, 1971, Bill Kilmer was a 31-year-old pro football veteran who had done little to distinguish himself in his pro career except nearly get killed in an automobile accident. In ten years of football, six as a San Francisco 49er and four as a New Orleans Saint, Kilmer had perhaps made less of a mark on the football fields of this country than a first-down stick.

In his six years with the 49ers, two of which he didn't even get into a game, he had thrown a total of 77 passes. He managed to put the ball into the air many more times in his four terms with the Saints, but he didn't seem to have much more success.

But on January 23, 1971, George Allen gave the Saints a reserve linebacker, Tom Roussel, and two draft picks (a fourth and an eighth), and the Saints gave Allen a well-used quarterback named Kilmer.

"Had I remained in Los Angeles and not come to Washington, I had made up my mind I wanted Bill Kilmer with the Rams," explained Allen, who made the deal only seventeen days after joining the Redskins. It was the first of eighteen trades he was to execute in his first seven months in the District of Columbia. "I've always had my eye on him. He did a job against us when he was with the Saints. We played them twice a year and they never should have been in the games. But Billy always made it close. His efforts with a mediocre team kept the games close."

At the same time, Allen was quick to point out that Kilmer would be the Redskins' backup quarterback, that Sonny Jurgensen still would be the team's No. 1 quarterback. After all, Jurgensen was considered one of the best passers, if not the best, in the league.

Then, two weeks before the start of the 1971 season, Jurgensen broke a bone in his left shoulder and Kilmer led the Redskins to their first post-season appearance in twenty-six years. And in case anyone saw that as a pure fluke, after Jurgensen ruptured an Achilles tendon midway through the 1972 season, Kilmer led the Redskins to the Super Bowl.

"The one thing I wanted to do was to bring a winner to Washington," said Jurgensen, a Redskin since 1964, "and I guess I did—by getting hurt."

No one accuses Kilmer of throwing a pass that goes rocketing to a receiver like Joe Namath's or that spirals 60 yards with the flick of a wrist like Jim Plunkett's. Yet the 6', 205-pound quarterback threw 19 touchdown passes in 1972, which was matched only by Namath.

There's more, though, to Kilmer than passing the ball or handing it off, an ingredient that probably is as vital as either of those.

"There's something about him," Allen says. "I don't know if it's charisma or whatever. It's a fierce determination to win and an ability to lead. Those are great qualities."

Even back when he was a Saint, this quality Allen talks about was noticeable, to the players, if not to the fans.

"I predict Bill will be the next Bobby Layne," cornerback Dave Whitsell said at one point. "Bill has the fellows thinking like winners [not an easy task with a team like the Saints]. If Kilmer jumped off a building, I believe the other guys would follow. He's that kind of leader—the same kind as Bobby Layne."

When Kilmer was an all-around back at UCLA, especially when he led the nation's colleges in total offense in 1960, many people believed he would soon lead some pro team to all sorts of championships. But after a fling at the trigger of San Francisco's shotgun offense in 1961, he didn't do any leading at all, unless it was to the corner bar. After a night in 1962, there was a chance that not only wouldn't he do any leading but also that he wouldn't do anything.

It was the night of December 5, and Kilmer was driving south on the Bayshore freeway south of San Francisco. He had spent a busy two days, hunting during the day and enjoying himself at night, then rushed back for practice, and he was tired, so tired that he feel asleep at the wheel.

His '57 Chevy convertible swerved off the road, careened about 450 feet through an empty field and came to a halt on its side in a ditch filled with mud and a foot or two of water.

"I woke up as I went off the road," Kilmer recalls. "I knew I didn't

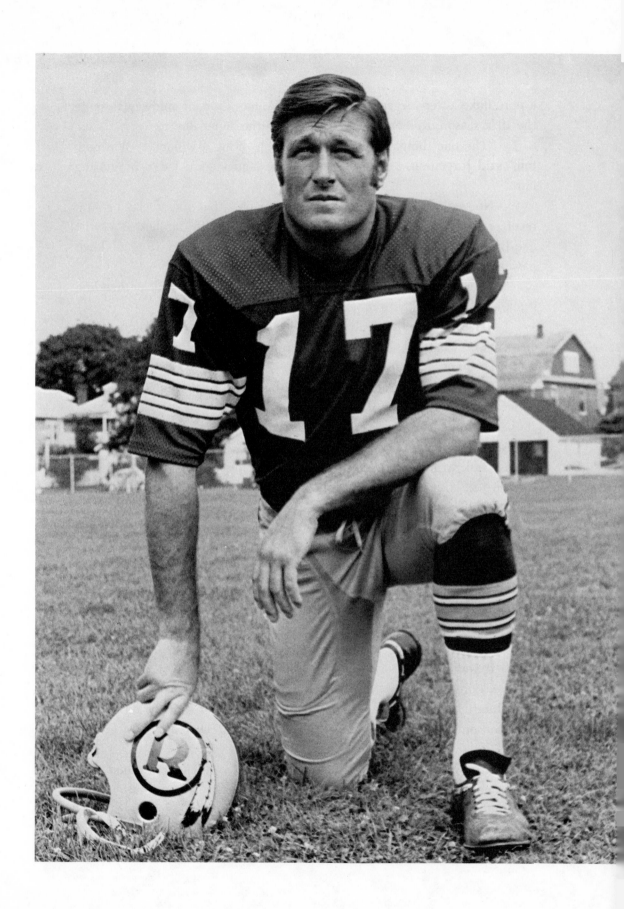

want to let go of the wheel and maybe get thrown out. If I went through the window or even the top, anything could have happened."

As the car hit the ditch, Kilmer's right leg got caught under the brake pedal and snapped ("I felt it snap and I could see the bone coming through"). Besides the compound fracture of the leg, he suffered a severely slashed chin, a deep gash over his right eye, a brain concussion and shock. A rescue squad cut through the top of the convertible, lifted Kilmer out and took him to a hospital, where he underwent surgery for four hours.

The worst, however, was not over. His leg had been immersed in the filthy water and there was a chance of serious infection. "The idea of amputation never really came up," Kilmer says. "They never came out and said anything, but they left the door open." The infection never set in, but the quarterback lay on his back in the hospital for twelve weeks, then returned in June for additional surgery in which bone chips were removed from the leg. The odds did not favor a return to football for Kilmer.

"My dad asked me if I knew what I was going to do," he relates. "He had a dry cleaning business and he put me to work while I decided. I worked two or three weeks behind one of those steam presses and I knew that was no life for me. I said pro football had to be easier.

"So I started getting ready, rehabilitating my leg. My life was athletics and I decided I was too young [twenty-three] to give it up. I'm really not that hard to persuade about things, especially if it's something I really want, and I really wanted this. Nobody had told me I couldn't play football any more. I had to prove to myself whether I could or I couldn't."

Kilmer didn't play at all in 1963, saw very little action in 1964 (14 passes, 36 rushes—he was tried at halfback) and then as third-string quarterback behind John Brodie and George Mira sat out the entire 1965 season. After throwing only 16 passes in 1966, he mercifully was placed on the expansion list and he was selected by New Orleans.

But even though he played a lot more as a Saint than as a 49er, he still hadn't found a place he could call home, because the Saints never seemed to be convinced that he was the quarterback they needed. Finally, Kilmer asked to be traded and that's when Allen entered his life. But Kilmer wasn't overjoyed at the thought of going to the Redskins.

"I wasn't happy about it at all," he says. "I obviously wasn't going to step right in and beat out Sonny Jurgensen, and I knew there were at least two or three clubs where I could play. I didn't want to be a backup quarterback."

So Kilmer did what seemed like the only smart thing—he asked Allen to trade him. If the coach had complied, it would have been the biggest regret in Kilmer's career, for Jurgensen fractured his shoulder trying to tackle Dick Anderson after the Miami safety intercepted a pass in the next-to-last exhibition game in 1971.

"I finished that game," Kilmer says, "and later George called me in. He said I had the job, that he had confidence in me. I said, 'Here's my chance.' I knew there could be no more talking, no more thinking. That wasn't going to do it."

Using passes when he needed them and calling plays smartly, as befits a veteran, Kilmer did it, sparking the Redskins into the playoffs, while Jurgensen got into only 5 games and threw 28 passes. Kilmer, meanwhile, emerged with one of the better passing records in the league, completing 54 percent of his throws for 2,221 yards.

"For years I've wanted just one break," he said at the time. "I wanted to work with a team that had a good offense and defense. This is what we have in Washington. I wasn't going to blow the opportunity. As long as I've waited I know second chances are hard to come by. Now I've got a team with great receivers like Jefferson, Taylor and Smith, runners like Larry Brown and Charley Harraway and a damned good offensive line as well. I've never had an offense like this—in high school, college or the pros. It's sensational."

The Redskin fans, long starved for a winner, thought Kilmer was sensational. That, however, didn't ensure the Californian the No. 1 job for 1972. After all, Jurgensen would be healthy again, and he had as much right to feel he was No. 1 as did Kilmer.

Before the battle could begin, though, Kilmer had to sign a contract. He had gone through the 1971 season without signing and when he was asked why, he said, "I had a unique opportunity to produce. I figured if I did a good job of helping the Redskins that in the end the money would fall into place. I couldn't have gotten any more by signing early. I had the cards in my hand, especially after Sonny got hurt. It was like filling an inside straight."

With the contract business out of the way, the business on the field began again and Allen had what coaches always insist is a happy dilemma —selecting a starting quarterback from two capable competitors. In some instances, a fight between two such quarterbacks could divide a team's loyalties. But not the Redskins.

"The name of the game is winning and whoever wins for us is the quarterback we want in there," said defensive back Mike Bass. Then he compared the two.

"Kilmer is the more vocal of the two, more brazen," he explained. "He's a throwback to Bobby Layne. He'll get the job done any way he can. This has to have its effect on the team. You can tell he wants to win so badly. You have to be behind a guy like that.

"Sonny is smooth, calculating, a great thinker on the field who does a superb job of throwing the ball and picking defenses apart. In doing this, he ignites the fire in the other players. On third-and-two, I'd rather have Kilmer; on third-and-ten, I'd rather have Jurgensen. That's the way I look at it."

The way Allen looked at it Kilmer was the No. 1 quarterback going into the season. But two victories and one loss later, he was No. 2.

"I knew the day we lost a game, I'd be replaced," Kilmer said after the New England Patriots pulled out a 24–23 upset. "When you don't win, you're replaced. But I've got to go ahead and prepare myself the same way I would if I was the starter. Who knows what's going to happen?"

Indeed, who knows? Kilmer and the rest of the Redskins found out on the fifteenth play of the seventh game of the season. Playing against the Giants in New York, Jurgensen ruptured an Achilles tendon and Kilmer was No. 1 again.

"Somebody said, 'Okay, Whiskey, you gotta do it now so let's get going,'" Kilmer related. And the Redskins went—directly to the Super Bowl.

"I feel badly for Sonny, honest to God," the thirty-three-year-old Kilmer said. "I didn't want the job this way, but that's my role with this club. You have to understand the nature of my job, the job of any No. 2 quarterback. When the No. 1 man gets hurt, you get thrown to the dogs. I'm not complaining. In fact, I love it."

Kilmer also liked the idea of knowing he had the No. 1 job the rest of the year.

"This has absolutely nothing to do with Sonny, but with him behind me I wouldn't take as many chances as maybe I should have," he said after Jurgensen's injury. "When you've got two guys fighting for a job, both of them are gonna be more conservative. Look what happened with

Sonny. Now I can be more freewheeling. I know I can throw an interception without being jerked right away. Psychologically, my position is different."

With the Redskins, his position has been the same as it was with his other clubs—quarterback. But he's been playing it differently, and it's certain that the 49ers and the Saints have noticed.

Daryle Lamonica

Some pro football players collect ten- and twenty-dollar bills. Others collect girls. Still others collect splinters. Daryle Lamonica collects mishaps.

He isn't as fond of his collection as most numismatists are of theirs, but he's stuck with it. He can't sell it or even give it away; all he can do is shove it into the deepest corner of a drawer somewhere, close the drawer tightly so it can't accidentally sneak out and forget it. And with admirable intensity and determination, Lamonica has done just that.

After all the mishaps that have struck the Oakland Raider quarterback, a weaker man would have turned in his movie projector and gone into another business, like rug weaving. But this man of Lamonica keeps overcoming both the nails and the boulders strewn in his path, keeps his head upright and keeps throwing passes that perennially carry the Raiders into the post-season playoffs.

Most of Lamonica's problems have been physical, and the fact that Joe Namath's knees attract more attention hasn't lessened the pain any for Daryle.

Take 1969, for example. Starting with an exhibition game against Kansas City and ending with the American League championship game against the same team, Lamonica suffered a wrist injury, a pulled hamstring, a torn muscle, an injured right shoulder, a virus that put him in the hospital the night before a game with San Diego, an injured left shoulder,

Brodie,
Hadl, and Bradshaw:
one thing
on their minds.

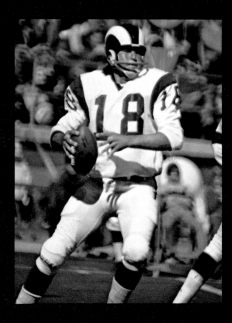

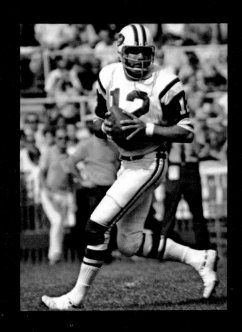

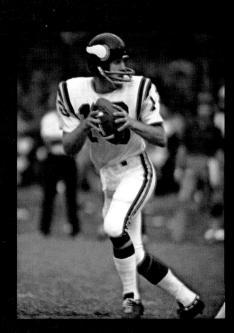

"The man."

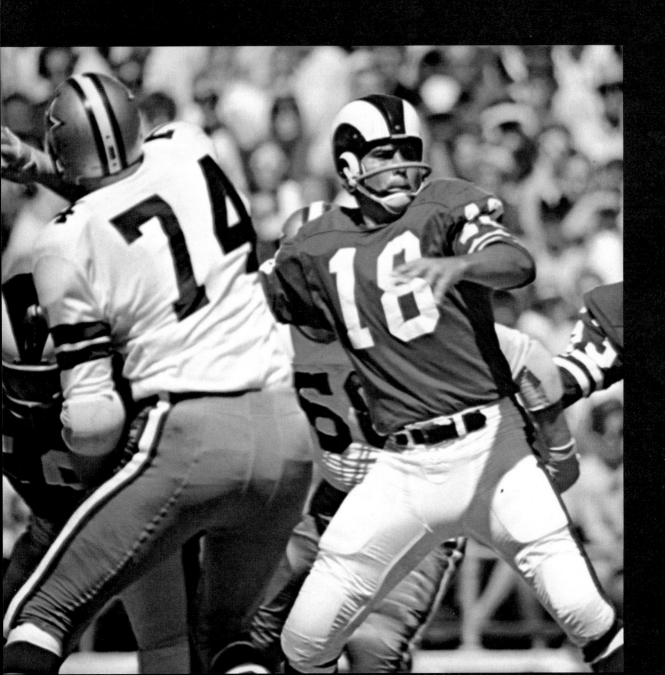

Bill Kilmer:
George is right,
we can do it.

(opposite page)
Bob Griese:
Inheriting the mantle.

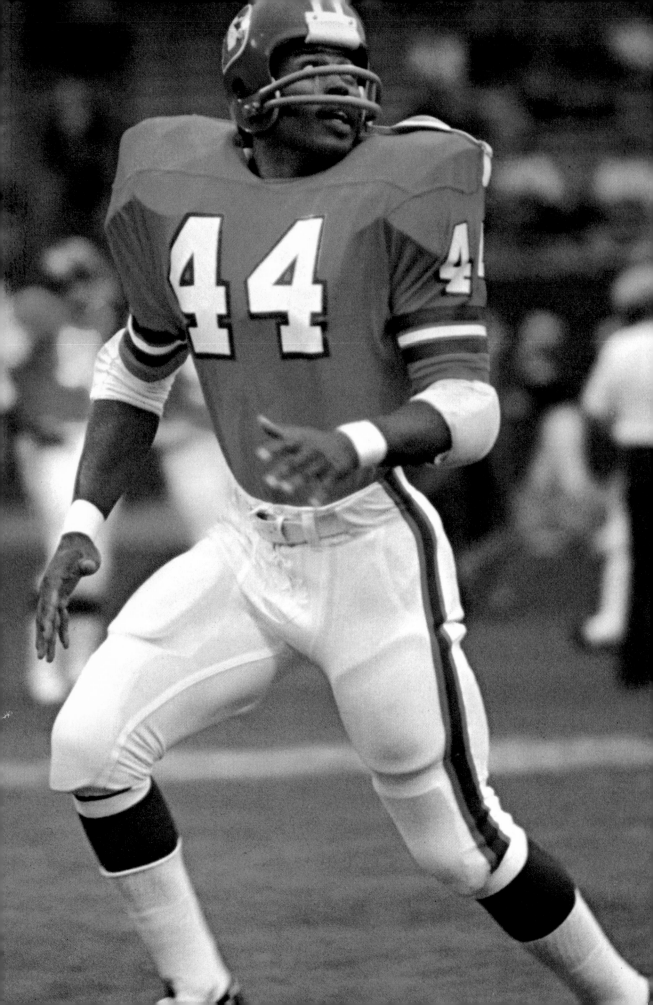

Jim Plunkett: They didn't seem this big in college.

Floyd Little: Keep your eye on the goal.

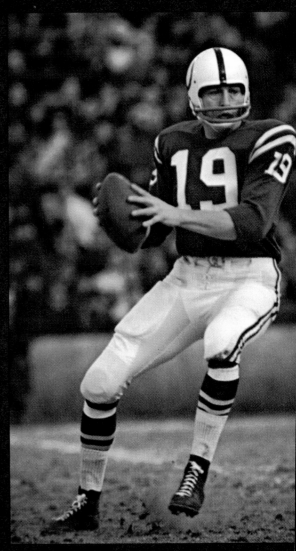

Dawson, Lamonica, Unitas,
and Namath: Year in, year out.

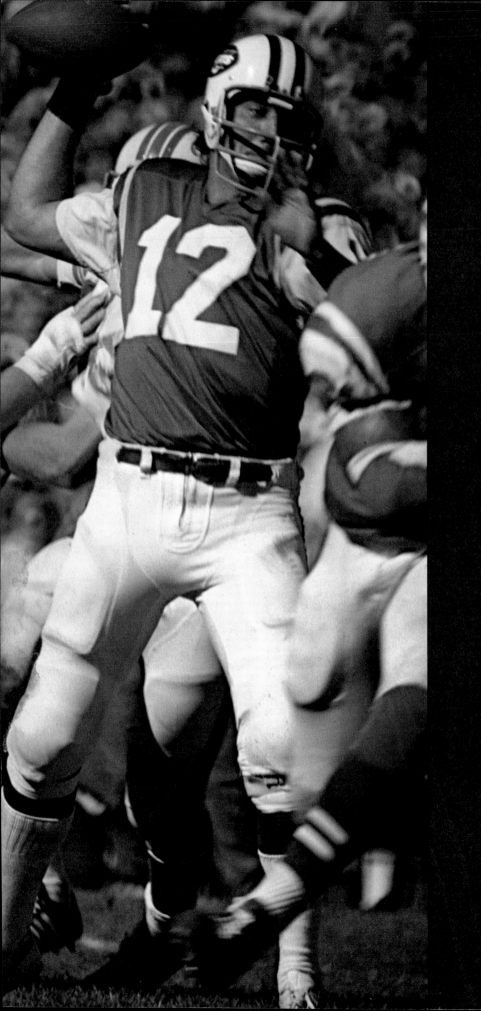

Namath and Butkus:
offense and defense.

Fran Tarkenton: Looking for number one.

bruised ribs, back muscle spasms that put him in the hospital the night before a game with Cincinnati and, finally, hand and wrist injuries. In other words, enough ailments to keep Marcus Welby busy for a whole season of television shows.

The next year, 1970, they wouldn't have had to worry about Welby reruns because they had Lamonica reruns instead: a strained knee, a separated shoulder, a jammed wrist, a badly bruised shoulder, back muscle spasms, sore hip, tennis elbow, bruised ankle, sprained neck, injured groin (the last wiping him out in a championship game for the second straight season).

In 1971, the 6'3", 215-pound graduate of Notre Dame decided that if variety was the spice of life, his life was spicy enough so he concentrated his efforts on one main injury—a hand ailment—but the problem cropped up in the opening game of the season and it bothered him severely enough the remainder of the year to become the focal point of post-season surgical action.

Throughout all the agony, though, Lamonica has lost none of his desire, none of his confidence, a confidence that enabled him to say once, "In a street fight, I'd probably hold my own with any human being."

It might take a street fight—with a gorilla, perhaps—to keep Lamonica out of a game; not much else can. In his first ten years as a pro, the son of a peach farmer missed only one regular-season game. That was in 1968 when a combination of back trouble and a hyperextended knee forced him to watch the Raiders' game with Denver from somewhere other than crouched behind the center. Of course, the doctor told him the injuries would keep him out of the next three games, but Lamonica returned the following week and Oakland won the game.

Although some observers might begin to get the idea that Lamonica is really a robot who's oblivious to all the ailments that cascade around his body, he's not that way at all. The repeated blows to his person occasionally penetrate the Xs and Os that dominate his thinking processes, but he appears to have a special set of antibodies that fight off the disease known as negative thinking.

"When you wake up some Monday mornings and find it hard to get out of bed, you think about it," he says. "You know, what am I doing in this profession? But give yourself two days' rest and you're ready. We're a breed of our own. I really am convinced of this. I know it's in my blood;

it's a great love and I've got a burning desire to play. I don't consider it a job. I play football because I love the game. I love the challenge and that's why I've never thought about hanging up the cleats.

"I know that some day there will come a time when I will have to hang my cleats up. I don't cherish the thought of that day. I will definitely play at least until I jeopardize my health. If I ever do jeopardize my health in any way, I'll probably retire, but I don't think of that time."

Instead, Lamonica thinks of the next title the Raiders will win. The last one they won was in 1967 when they were the champions of the old AFL. Lamonica was the Most Valuable Player in the league that year, just as he was in 1969 when the Raiders lost to Kansas City in the AFL title game. In those two years, as well as the one in between, Lamonica threw for well over 3,000 yards each season and averaged 30 touchdown tosses.

That was a marked difference from the previous four years when he played behind Jack Kemp at Buffalo. He appeared in every Bill game in those years, but his total passes for that entire period fell well short of the number he threw in any of his first four terms with Oakland.

In going to Buffalo from Notre Dame, the Fresno, California, native made the transition for not much more than the eighty-five-cent phone call it took the Baltimore Colts to get Johnny Unitas.

"The Bills offered me $10,000 to sign," recalls Lamonica, a 24th-round draft choice in 1963, "but I got real smart. I decided to ask for $12,000 and sign for $11,000. They gave me $12,000 without another word. When I was later practicing for the East-West game, I learned that free agents were signing for $15,000."

Thus, Lamonica was not the richest man ever to play pro football. Nor, in his first four years, was he the busiest.

"I realize a coach must stay with one quarterback to get the most out of his system," he says. "That's the way pro ball is. But I was confident in Buffalo that I could do the job. So I phoned the coach [Joe Collier] and I told him that for the following season I wanted assurance I'd be given an equal opportunity to try for the first-string job."

Lamonica received no assurance, but shortly afterward he did receive news of a trade, one that sent him to Oakland in a four-player, three-draft choice transaction. The trade also sent him into the arms of Al Davis, perhaps the most secretive man in the NFL but also one of the smartest.

"I think that Al is the big reason I became an Oakland Raider,"

Lamonica says. "I think that he probably saw things in me that he liked—at least I like to believe that—but to me, Al Davis, without a doubt, has the greatest football mind in the business."

But while that mind helped build one of the most successful teams in the game, it hasn't figured out a way to keep Lamonica healthy. For example, there was no way the mind could get between Lamonica's right hand and Aaron Brown's helmet early in the third quarter of the 1969 AFL title game against Kansas City.

The game was tied 7–7 when Lamonica injured his hand on his follow-through on a pass. The quarterback left the game for eight minutes in that quarter, replaced by George Blanda, but he returned in an effort to avert a 17–7 loss. He could do very little, though, with a severely bruised wrist and three damaged fingers, and he wound up completing as many passes to Kansas City receivers—3—as he did to his own receivers in the 18 passes he threw after the injury.

"I could grip the ball, but I couldn't put any zip on it," he said.

Bizarrely, the injury was a repeat of the one he had suffered in the opening exhibition game that season, also against the Chiefs and also when his hand struck Aaron Brown's helmet on a follow-through.

"The doctor told me to put it in a cast for six weeks and rest it," Lamonica recalls. "But I told him I could maybe give it forty-eight hours rest. This is the way I make a living, throwing a football, and I can't throw a football with my hand in a cast."

He can't throw passes very well with a virus and a 102-degree temperature, but he did just that against San Diego that year. After spending the previous night in the hospital and getting out by deviously faking his temperature, he completed 19 of 26 passes, 3 for touchdowns, as the Raiders defeated the Chargers, 24–12.

He can't throw passes very well either with muscle spasms in his back, but he did against Cincinnati a few weeks later. Another hospital stay was called for, and this time he got out only after a doctor "cracked" his back ("I couldn't even get out of bed," he says). Playing with heat pads on his back and running up and down the sideline to keep loose when he wasn't in the game, Lamonica hit on 11 of 22 tosses, again 3 for touchdowns, and Oakland whipped the Bengals, 37–17.

Lest it be thought that Lamonica's favorite pastime is suffering injuries, it should be noted that away from the field, his favorite pursuit is the pursuit of animals. He pursues them as nearby as California and as far away as Africa.

"Some guys enjoy playing golf; some guys will sit in a bar or enjoy the big nightlife," Lamonica says. "But my way of unwinding after a game is going hunting for deer or duck shooting."

But that type of hunting is dessert for the Raider marksman; the main course is the type of hunting one finds in Africa.

"I guess I love the chase and the challenge," says Lamonica, who a few years ago went on a safari to Africa. "When I bagged a lion, it was a thrill I can't describe. It cost me $8,000 for that safari, but it was worth more. I realize a lot of people don't like killing. But a true sportsman doesn't look at killing in the strictest sense. No one really enjoys killing. It's the challenge, the excitement."

In a sense, Lamonica sees a similarity between hunting and playing football. "In stalking an animal," he says, "everything is a challenge, and this is basically the same thing you try to do to an opponent. You try to outwit him. You try to get any advantage that you can and put it on your side. I think when it all boils down, it's probably all basically the same. You have to have a game plan for an opponent and you have to have a game plan for the prey that you're after."

Prey, in a way, is how Lamonica looks at his opponents. He's the killer and they're his prey.

"Every athlete has to have a killer instinct," he says. "You've got to have that to play this game well. If a professional doesn't have it, he shouldn't be a professional. Striving to be the best at your position, playing to the best of your ability—these are the things I would call having a killer instinct.

"The quarterback has to have it more so than others. This is part of his game. He's the leader. He spends long hours in excess of what the other players do, breaking down the films with the coaches, studying the game plan, helping make up the game plan. This is a quarterback's job. He calls the plays and he starts the plays. This is his job alone. You have to be confident, know what you're doing at all times. You've got to grab the bull by the horns, so to speak, and be prepared. Without this, chances of having a winning ball club aren't too good.

"If you want to put this killer instinct in another term, it would be a competitor. I've always been a competitor. I've always wanted to win.

This is what I work for and I know if somebody beats me on a particular day I have another shot at them and it will be a different story."

This is the confidence, the determination that enables Lamonica to keep coming back. No matter how many injuries he's suffered, he has returned with even greater determination to stay healthy and win, and not necessarily in that order. To be sure, it takes a lot of determination to overcome the frustration Lamonica has experienced.

"Talk about being frustrated," he said after a groin injury knocked him out of the 1970 American Conference championship game against Baltimore in the second quarter. "You play and work from July to get in a game like that and you wind up watching it from the sidelines."

Nothing, it seems, can keep Lamonica on the sidelines for long.

Joe Namath

The Oakland Raiders kept hearing stories about how the arm and image of Joe Namath were in decline, but when the game was over, they were certain someone had been putting them on.

"I heard all this stuff about Joe slipping and all that," John Madden, the red-headed Oakland coach, said. "Well, if he's slipping, it's only on the grass. We don't have to face Namath again in 1972 and thank God for that."

Actually, it was Pete Rozelle and his jolly schedule makers Madden could thank, but no matter. He and his raiders had seen enough of Namath for one season and perhaps two. The Raiders, to be sure, won the game, 24–16, but they weren't convinced the victory was theirs until they were safely nestled in their Oakland Coliseum locker room, the locked door impenetrable and secure from the bullets and bombs of the wondrous wizard called Joe Namath.

In trying to keep the New York Jets in the playoff picture in this next-to-last game of the season, the long-haired, slope-shouldered quarterback unleashed 46 passes, completing 25 for 403 yards. He also had 2 intercepted, but that didn't dilute the Raiders' awed reaction to him.

"I found myself looking at the game like a fan," Bob Brown, Oakland's 280-pound all-pro offensive tackle, said after the onslaught. "I mean I was standing there on the sidelines in total awe of the guy. He was like a magician. He's unreal. He keeps his club in the game right up until that man shoots the .22 in the air."

This, perhaps, is Namath's most amazing ability. Given a chance to get his hands on the ball before the gun ends the game, he always has to be given a chance to win it. In this game, for instance, the Jets trailed by 8 points but had the ball on Oakland's 10-yard line (after a 45-yard pass to Jerome Barkum on fourth-and-31) with 59 seconds to play.

"It wasn't out of the question yet," Namath explained. "If we had scored quickly then and gotten an onside kick, we could have pulled it out."

Those aren't simply empty words coming from a loser's mouth. They are the words of a man who believes he can pull off that sort of thing at any moment and in any situation, and frequently, such as in the 1969 Super Bowl, he does. This time, however, it wasn't to be as Barkum dropped a pass in the end zone and Namath was sacked for a loss. The Jets wound up at the 6-yard line and 20 seconds later, the game ended, much to the relief of the ragged Raiders.

"Sure I'm tired," Willie Brown, the excellent cornerback, said, slumped on the bench in front of his locker. "Wouldn't you be tired if a guy ran you up and down the field like that? We knew he'd come out throwing and we gave him every coverage we had in the book. One time in the fourth quarter we had six defensive backs in the game. We would have used more, but that's all we carry on the roster."

That Namath pulled off such a potent performance was even more remarkable when it's considered that the Jets had a virtually nonexistent running attack that game. Injuries reduced the running backs to 15 carries throughout the entire game, and the Raiders knew they could concentrate all their defensive efforts on Namath.

Earlier in the same season, the Baltimore Colts concentrated on the large nose and strong arm of Namath, but they emerged in even less fortunate shape than the Raiders. In that contest, the fabled Johnny Unitas performed more than well enough to win—he completed 26 of 44 passes for 376 yards and 2 touchdowns. But Namath, piercing the Colts' presumably impregnable zone defense like a brick being hurled through a window, amassed an incredible 496 yards (third highest total in NFL history) and fired 6 touchdown passes, 1 short of the league mark, in completing 15 of 28 tosses.

In the first quarter, Namath combined with Eddie Bell on a 65-yard pass play for the Jets' first touchdown. The second, third and fourth came in rapid succession, all in the second quarter and all within one minute and 29 seconds. First was a 67-yard play to John Riggins, then came a 28-yarder with Don Maynard and finally there was a 10-yard strike to Richard Caster.

Joe rested his bazooka that passes for an arm in the third quarter, but in the fourth it became obvious what he was saving his energy for—a 79-yard touchdown toss to Caster and, for good measure, an 80-yard bomb to Caster. That last score could have been construed as Namath's way of rubbing it in, but he was only protecting the Jets' three-point lead.

"Waiting for the kickoff [after Unitas's second scoring pass]," Namath related, "I was thinking about another long pass to Caster on the first play, but I wasn't sure I should risk it, only three points ahead. But then I said to myself, 'If you ain't confident, you don't belong here.' So I decided to try to score again."

Namath was successful in that effort, just as he is in many things he does on the football field, but his success doesn't surprise him. He's come to expect it.

"I get paid for it," says the 6'2", 195-pound superstar whose $500,000 contract for 1972–73 made him the highest paid player in NFL history. "I'm supposed to do the job. It's cut and dried. I'm convinced I'm better than anybody else. I've been convinced of that for quite a while. I haven't seen anything out there that I couldn't do and do well. When you go back to guys like Sammy Baugh, guys like that, they were great, sure, but it wasn't the game it is now. Johnny Unitas has been great, but I just like to believe I'm better."

There are times, though, that even Namath is found to be human, susceptible to colds, interceptions, broken bones and stingy defenses.

For example, in spite of his picturesque performances against Baltimore and Oakland in 1972, Namath had difficulty at times penetrating some of the defenses he faced. He acknowledged that some of the interceptions he threw were the result of foolish moves by him, but he also pointed to the kind of problems that even Cupid would have if he took two years off from shooting arrows.

"I've been away from certain situations for so long that sometimes I am slow at adjusting to them," Namath explained.

Namath was away not because he wanted to be but because he did some silly things, such as breaking a wrist and tearing knee ligaments. He broke his right wrist on October 18, 1970, when he was slammed to the ground by Billy Ray Smith, a Baltimore defensive tackle, and in his first

game after that, an exhibition contest against Detroit on August 7, 1971, he severely damaged his left knee while trying to make a tackle after a fumble.

The wrist injury was something that could happen to any quarterback, but his fourth knee operation could have been avoided if he hadn't tried to tackle Mike Lucci after the Lions' linebacker recovered a fumble by Lee White, a Jet running back. But Namath isn't the kind of quarterback who tries not to do anything.

"You're too good a football player," Ken Meyer, a Jet assistant coach, told him as he hobbled around the locker room. "If you weren't, you would have let Lucci go."

And so it was that from the first exhibition game to the eleventh regular-season contest Namath sat around, then ran around, until he was ready for his second return in four months. The return could have been mistaken for the Second Coming. The reaction of both his Jet teammates and his Jet fans revealed all there is to know about the esteem in which Namath is held.

"Forget Woodstock. Forget the blackout of '65. Joe Willie is here," wrote a 19-year-old fan to *The New York Times* after she soared from her seat at Shea Stadium into a state of euphoria. "We are united for 2½ hours in sports. They lost the game, but we feel as if we've just conquered the world. This is the center of the universe now, and nothing Ali or Frazier or Seaver or Tarkenton or Lindsay ever does from now on will even come close to the spiritual uplift Broadway Joe is giving to us 64,000 Jet fans. Somebody stole, or I left, my transistor radio at Shea, yeah. I came away with an unforgettable charismatic experience."

The way the fans reacted when they saw Namath trot onto the field to replace the injured Bob Davis in the second quarter of that game against San Francisco, it appeared they were having an orgasmic experience. They reacted to his every move and went especially wild when he threw three touchdown passes that just fell short of overcoming San Francisco leads of 17–0 and 24–7.

"I never heard anything like it," said Earlie Thomas, a Jet cornerback. "Usually, I tune out the crowd, but this was the first time at Shea Stadium I ever heard it. It was electrifying. All that night I couldn't sleep. It wasn't the excitement of the game; it was the roar of the crowd. I kept hearing that roar over and over."

But it's not only the fans who are turned on by Namath; it's also his teammates, and the first to admit it is Davis, the man who had to content himself with second-string status after Namath's return.

"There may be a better quarterback some day, but there will never be a better figure in sports. Whoever plays quarterback in New York after him never will be able to replace him. It's like the guy who replaced Babe Ruth in right field. You know, the only guy you can compare Joe to is Babe Ruth."

When Namath is at quarterback for the Jets, the blockers block better and the pass catchers catch better. He instills them with something extra that makes them better football players. The blockers have an extra incentive. With Namath's knees in worse condition than a West Virginia coal mine, they know they have to keep the defensive behemoths away from him; the life they save may be theirs as well as Namath's.

"You can't afford to let anyone get to him," says John Riggins, the Jets' fine running back. "He's like a diamond. You don't want to scratch it up. You want to keep it as shiny as you can."

This particular diamond began polishing himself in the small western Pennsylvania town of Beaver Falls, where he was born May 31, 1943. A number of people added a little polish to Namath as he grew up, including his high school football coach, Larry Bruno.

"My high school football coach said something to the team once," Namath recalls. "He told us, 'If you don't dream about it, it won't happen.' I've dreamed about things and a lot of them have come true. I don't think I'd rather have done anything different than I did—except maybe for some of the bad things when I was a kid. I've always stayed active. One of the things I strive for is keeping versatile. I look for things to do."

Namath has done many things in his still young life, both on and off the field. He's become the most magnetic name in pro football, he's appeared in movies, he's dated Raquel Welch, he's lent his name to businesses that have failed, he's been involved in a controversial night spot, he's helped build what was once one of the weakest football franchises into one of the strongest, he's retired from the game and returned and he's developed the most famous knees in the history of the American Medical Association.

Joe Namaths don't come along too often; perhaps none ever will again. As Sonny Werblin, the man who signed Joe to his original $427,000 contract out of Alabama, has said, "He is a product of his time."

An integral part of his time was the war between two professional football leagues. Namath's lucrative and storied contract helped give the American League stature, and his guaranteed victory over the Baltimore Colts in the 1969 Super Bowl gave the league instant parity with the big brother National League.

Now, in spite of his fragile knees, no matter what group is polled —coaches, scouts, fans—the majority replies "Namath" when asked which quarterback they would take if they had their choice of all the quarterbacks playing today. Opposing defensive players, of course, are the ones who have to contend with Namath first-hand, and they also are first to recognize the threat he represents every time his white Pumas step behind the center.

"Joe has great leadership qualities," says Bruce Taylor, a San Francisco defensive back. "All of his teammates look up to him. Whenever he's in there, they put out 200 percent. The big problem defending against Namath is that he throws the ball a lot. He keeps coming at you."

And coming and coming and coming.

Jim Plunkett

As the bus rolled along the Penn-Lincoln Parkway, carrying the New England Patriots to Greater Pittsburgh Airport, Charlie Gogolak tried to push his seat back into a reclining position and the seat made a sharp, loud noise.

Startled by the sudden sound, Jim Plunkett sat up quickly. Then, after determining what it was, he relaxed again.

"I'm getting gun-shy even on buses," he said.

Plunkett's feeling was understandable. In the previous few hours, the young Patriot quarterback had been dumped six times by the Pittsburgh Steelers for losses totaling 72 yards. Besides picking up a lot of dirt on the seat of his pants, he also had acquired a dandy black eye, a memento from Dwight White, a 250-pound defensive end who figured out how to penetrate Plunkett's double-barred helmet with his rock-hard forearm.

"It seems like I'm getting hurt more this year," Plunkett said after the 33–3 loss to the Steelers in the middle of the 1972 season. "I got hit last year and I got right back up. This year I get knocked down and sometimes I don't get up so quick."

Physical bruises, though, weren't the only problems bothering the second-year pro; psychological bruises were present as well, and they hurt even worse.

"You can bounce back after being beat up and sore, but the frustration of losing lingers," he said. "There's a lot of frustration in this game and it's tough to cope with. Not winning is the biggest frustration of all. You figure that being the quarterback, you shoulder a lot of the responsibility for what happens and you figure you can help the team more than any other individual by coming up with the big plays. But for some reason I'm not doing it. I can't figure out why not and it gets to you. I get tired every week of having to explain what happened. You can't help but feel badly."

Plunkett felt bad on eleven of the fourteen Sundays the Patriots played in 1972 because that's how many times they lost. Moreover, the pain was particularly excruciating nine of those times because the Patriots allowed more than 30 points on those occasions, which can be insurmountable odds for even Joe Namath or Bob Griese to overcome.

"It's very hard to beat teams that score 38 and 41 points against you," he said at one painful point. "You get frustrated in a game like that. When you get behind by a touchdown, it isn't bad. But when you fall behind by two, then I've got to throw and the other team knows it. It becomes that much harder. The opposition puts on a three-man rush and everyone else is back there covering.

"Sometimes I find myself trying to do it all myself and realistically it can't be done. If we fall behind early, it just puts too much pressure on everybody. I really feel it sometimes. I even suffered a loss of confidence for a short time. I reached a mental low, but I bounced back and I'm playing better than earlier in the season."

With a team that has the weaknesses of the Patriots, it sometimes can be difficult to tell just how good a Plunkett is. It would be silly to suggest that he was all good while the other Patriots were all bad. Plunkett, in fact, is the first to admit when he's not playing well, as he did toward the end of the disastrous season of 1972 when he said, "None of us are having a very good year and I'm included. I'm not playing well, and my not playing well is affecting the rest of the team."

Whatever Plunkett does—good or bad—has a monumental effect on the Patriots because he is the foundation on which the team is being built. Since it very likely will take a while for that construction job to be completed, it would be wise to encase the foundation in glass, or at least to put up "Do not touch" signs. But somehow that wouldn't work in pro football, which means Plunkett must continue to suffer all the slings and arrows of outrageously large defensive linemen.

Billy Sullivan, the Patriots' president, could have saved Plunkett from his present fate if he had listened to all the teams that wanted to give him king-sized quantities of players and draft choices in exchange for his No. 1 draft pick in 1971. There were some teams among the many for whom Plunkett conceivably could be winning championships today. But none of the offers intrigued Sullivan enough, and to this day he doesn't regret retaining the prize pick and picking the prize quarterback.

Most team officials would be satisfied to compare a young quarterback like Plunkett with John Unitas, but when Sullivan speaks of Plunkett, he is not so parochial; his views exceed the confines of football.

"I'll never get over on the day of the draft how Plunkett handled so many questions," Sullivan says, "some of which to me were the most insulting, degrading, unbelievably stupid questions I'd never heard. Yet he took them all in stride. I know I couldn't have done it and I've been answering questions a lot of years. He reminded me in poise of Jack Kennedy. I don't think anyone ever handled himself before questions as well as Jack Kennedy and I never thought we'd see his likeness. I think Jim has a chance in that area. I have the feeling that somewhere in the ranks of football there will emerge a President of the United States and this is the type of boy who can do it."

Whether or not quarterback Plunkett ever becomes President Plunk-

ett, his story still is one of the more fascinating in sports. A Mexican-American, Jim was born on December 5, 1947, to Carmen and William Plunkett in San Jose, California. Both his parents were blind and had met at a school for the blind in New Mexico. His mother became blind as the result of an illness at about the age of twenty; his father, who died in 1969, was afflicted with progressive blindness. Aided by welfare, his father supported the family (there were two older girls) by selling newspapers in San Jose.

Jim was an outstanding high school athlete, but in the summer before he was to take that ability to Stanford, doctors discovered a tumor on the left side of his neck that they feared might be cancerous. The thyroid tumor, however, proved benign, and all it cost Plunkett was a late start in freshman football.

That was enough, though, to hamper his effectiveness at quarterback and prompt Coach John Ralston to suggest that he switch to defensive end. "I am a quarterback," Plunkett told Ralston and then set about to prove it, throwing hundreds of passes each day during the summer.

Ralston became convinced that Plunkett should remain a quarterback, but he red-shirted him, or held him out of varsity play during his sophomore year. There was no holding him back after that, though, and the 6'3", 210-pound Plunkett went on to set a bushel of national conference and school records. He capped his collegiate career by setting another record that can't be found in any book, a record for unselfishness.

As is the case with red-shirted players, they are eligible for the pro draft when their original college class graduates. That meant Plunkett could have decided not to play his final year at Stanford but instead declare himself available for the draft. He would have been a high draft choice and he would have commanded a lot of money for signing. But two thoughts dissuaded him from taking that route.

First, he thought of his teammates who had been working with him toward the goal of all Pacific-8 Conference players—to reach the Rose Bowl. Second, he thought of the Chicano kids he worked with and whom he was attempting to show that there was something beyond ghetto life. "How could I tell them not to drop out of high school if it looked like I was dropping out of Stanford?" he pondered.

So Plunkett passed up the draft, stayed in school and led Stanford to the Rose Bowl, where he completed 20 of 30 passes in a stunning 27–17 upset of powerful Ohio State. He also won the Heisman Trophy and as he looked forward to his pro career, he said, "I would like to start immediately. I certainly don't want to come up to the pros and sit on the bench. You can't win there."

Never, though, in his boldest moments of fantasizing about his future did he imagine what actually would happen to him. He couldn't even imagine it when he arrived at the Patriots' camp in 1971.

"First of all, when I came in, Joe Kapp was there, and when that changed [Kapp left in a contract dispute], Mike Taliaferro was still there," Plunkett recalls. "I figured they'd play me behind Mike and when the opportunity arose they would gradually put me in, like if we were way behind in a game or way ahead."

But Plunkett wasn't the ordinary rookie coming into a pro camp and trying to win a job as a reserve quaterback. While at Stanford, he had received a pro education from John Brodie of the San Francisco 49ers. "Jim has a better concept of the game than a lot of pro quarterbacks playing the game today," Brodie said when Plunkett still was at Stanford. "A college quarterback with his talents doesn't come along very often."

It's not too often either that a quarterback comes along and plays every offensive play of every game his team plays in the regular season; in fact, it never had happened in NFL history. But that's precisely what Plunkett did—as a rookie.

"I picked up the last two pre-season games and then they just gave me the position," he says. "They stuck with me right or wrong. Even if we were behind, they left me in there. I never had to worry. I didn't have to worry about being taken out. There was a lot more security for me in the way they handled my situation than for other quarterbacks. If I had sat on the bench, I wouldn't have progressed as rapidly as I have."

There were, however, progression pains, such as the confusion of plays. Once, for example, he called a Green Right formation, which was fine at Stanford but which the Patriots didn't have in their playbook. Or the 36-P play he called in an audible, only to realize later that he meant P-36, an entirely different play.

"Sometimes," h eadds, "we'd go into a game with ten running plays and I'd forget 3 or 4 of them during the game and I just stuck with the ones I remembered."

But John Mazur, the New England coach in Plunkett's rookie year, never panicked. "He let me go on my own pretty much," the quarterback explains, "unless I got in a real deep hole and couldn't get out. Then he'd help. He sent in no more than five plays a game. In some games he didn't send in a single play. This helped me mature faster."

Plunkett matured so quickly that in his first league game, he led the Patriots to a 20–6 upset of the Oakland Raiders. "That gave me more satisfaction than winning the Rose Bowl," he says. "It's like your first love affair. You never forget it."

The Patriots won five more games that season, including other upsets over Miami and Baltimore, and emerged with a record no one ever thought they could achieve. A primary reason they did achieve it was the 19 touchdown passes Plunkett threw, including an 88-yarder that downed Baltimore in the final game of the season.

"I was a little nervous when I called that play," he admits, "but I did call it. Earlier in the year, I wouldn't have." That's the tipoff on the progress Plunkett made in that first season. The more he saw he could do, the more confident he became.

"Once you've gained experience and confidence, you're not afraid to take a chance," he said as he prepared to begin his second season. "I'll take more chances this year. There will be times I'll suddenly see something and decide to go for the bomb and get burned for it. But I'm more confident about throwing deep."

That prompted Plunkett to recall a situation in his first year when his conservative nature showed through.

"It was against San Francisco and we had just recovered a fumble on their 25," he related. "So what did I do? I called two running plays, threw a short pass and we had the field goal blocked. We got nothing. What I really wanted to do was use this special play we have [a delay pass to tight end], but frankly, I didn't have the guts to call it."

To play behind the porous line the Patriots have had and to try and counter the defensive problems they've also had takes a lot of guts and determination. But his teammates know Plunkett has those ingredients.

"Jim is the key to our success," place kicker Charlie Gogolak said at one point. "He's going to have to pass well, call all the plays and be the leader. That's an awful lot of pressure, but Jim is a stable guy. I'm glad it's all on his shoulders and not on somebody else's."

The shoulders are broad and strong, strong enough for a team to build on.

Fran Tarkenton

"Sometimes," Fran Tarkenton once said, "I wake up in the middle of the night and shudder at the thought that I might never do anything meaningful in the game, might never win even a division title for all the years of trying. Plenty of good players go through an entire football career and never win a championship, and to me this is tragic."

Tarkenton expressed that feeling shortly after the Minnesota Vikings traded him to the New York Giants in 1967. He had begun his pro life in 1961, the same year the Vikings began life as a National Football League expansion team, and the closest he got to his title ambition was in 1964 when the Vikings finished in a tie for second in their division.

In going to the Giants, Tarkenton knew he wasn't going to a champion because his new team had won only ten games the previous three years. But he thought in time the Giants could build themselves back to the status they held in the late fifties and early sixties, when they were perennial champions of some kind. It wasn't to be, though, because the closest he got with the Giants was second place.

Then came his second trade. This time the Giants sent him back to the Vikings, and on that day in 1972, Tarkenton rejoiced because now, finally, he was going to get his elusive championship. After all, the Vikings had won their division crown the last four seasons—four of the five years Tarkenton was gone from their lineup—and they had the stingiest and roughest defense in the league. All they needed was a competent quarterback and they would win not only their division title but also the Super Bowl championship that had eluded them.

And Tarkenton certainly was more than a competent quarterback. In his eleven seasons as a pro, he had become one of the five most prolific passers of all time and had built a reputation as one of the shrewdest quarterbacks in the game. Statistically, he had completed nearly 55 percent of his passes for 28,484 yards and 216 touchdown passes, and he had been intercepted only 4.4 percent of all the times he threw the ball. Here, surely, was the man who could serve as the missing link, the man who would solidify the Vikings as the NFL's next super team.

So the Vikings won only half their games, seven, lost the same number, finished third in their division and once again Tarkenton was without a championship.

To be sure, the veteran quarterback was one of the most successful passers in the league in 1972, hitting on 215 of 371 passes for a 58 percent completion record, 2,651 yards and 18 touchdowns. He also had the lowest interception percentage, 3.5, in the National Conference. But, contrary to what the Vikings had believed, Tarkenton's passing wasn't enough because the defense suddenly fell apart and in no way resembled the unit that had become the scourge of the league. Whereas in the previous two seasons, the Vikings had allowed a total of 282 points, in 1972 they permitted 252. In the end, Minnesota lost three games by three points each, two games by two points each and its hold on the division crown.

Thus, if Tarkenton were to experience the thrill of playing on a champion, it would have to be in his thirteenth or fourteenth or seventeenth season, if ever. "If I played for a team for fifteen years without winning a championship," he has said, "I'd be the first guy to show up at training camp for the sixteenth year."

Despite his ill fortune at not playing on a title team, Tarkenton remains one of the most celebrated quarterbacks in the game. He is one of the smallest—6', 190 pounds—but he also is one of the healthiest, never having missed a game because of an injury. That record is all the more incredible because he's been one of the most active and fearless quarterbacks in the game, running with the ball whenever he has deemed it necessary and not only "out of sheer terror," as his first coach, Norm Van Brocklin, did when he served as one of the outstanding quarterbacks in the NFL.

Many people, in fact, believe Francis Asbury Tarkenton, son of a Methodist minister, was the prototype for the running quarterbacks who have emerged in the pro game in recent years. Having started scrambling as a way of life—his—and as a means of staying away from mammoth oncoming tacklers in the Vikings' early years, Tarkenton soon became known as the Scrambler, someone who many observers felt would rather run than pass.

As successful as he was at the maneuver, it soon became a stigma that would stay with him as long as he couldn't lead a team to a championship. "Scrambling quarterbacks don't win championships," said Van Brocklin, who had been the classic drop back, pocket passer.

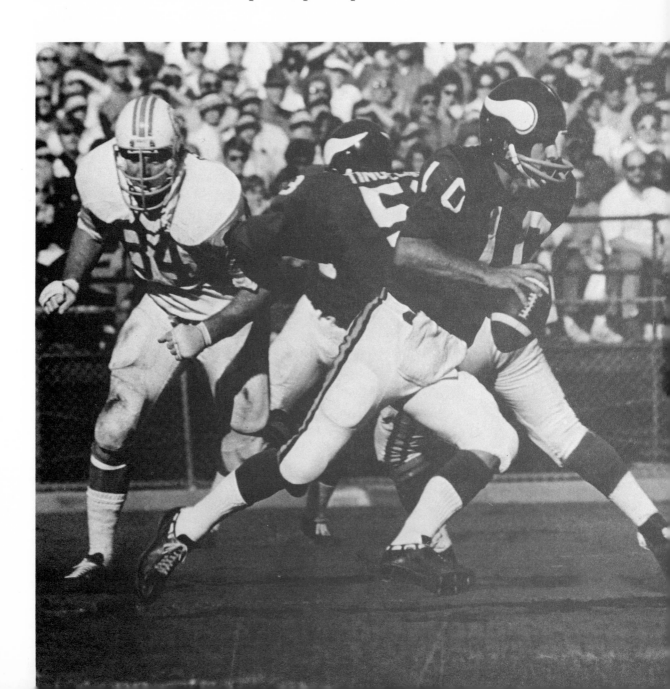

Tarkenton, of course, always has resented the suggestion that he cares more about scrambling than passing and he especially scoffs at the idea that the kind of running he does is any different from the running employed by such people as Roger Staubach and Greg Landry.

"It's difficult to characterize quarterbacks," the Georgian says. "It used to be very simple. If a quarterback dropped back seven yards every time, people would call him a pocket quarterback. But even the pocket quarterback ran the ball some. You look back at Unitas and Starr in their heyday. They would run the ball 30-35 times a year out of the pocket.

"Some quarterbacks may run more than others, some may scramble more than others, depending on what you want to call scrambling or running. When I used to run up the middle years ago, that was called scrambling. When Greg Landry runs up the middle now, he's called a running quarterback. The coaches are paranoid about daring to call their quarterback a scrambler because in the past they probably said you can't ever win with a scrambler.

"The important thing isn't whether a team can win with a running quarterback, but whether the quarterback has a team around him. It's not important whether you're a pocket quarterback or a scrambler. For years I just happened to be the only person anyone would ever call a scrambler."

Throughout his years in the NFL, Tarkenton has been called worse things, too—by the defensive linemen who have to chase him while he's scrambling around in the backfield and by the defensive backs who have to try to cover the receivers while he's running around waiting for one of them to get free.

"That damned Tarkenton," Erich Barnes, a former Cleveland defensive back, once said. "He runs like he's in a basketball game. He takes the skill away from a defensive back. He makes you cover a man for five or six seconds and that's a long time. Once the first pattern is over, you're fighting for your life."

"You want to kill him when you get hold of him—if you get hold of him," said Ed O'Bradovich, former Chicago end. "His quickness is unbelievable. Just when you think you've got him, he wheels around across the field. And the next thing you know, he's coming back at you."

Lamar Lundy, who was an outstanding tackle with Los Angeles, once compared the pursuit of Tarkenton to "a farm boy chasing a greased pig. By the time you catch it, you're so dang tired you can't have any fun with it."

Looking at the situation from Tarkenton's side, Tommy Mason, a former teammate, said it was akin to a backyard touch game. "Francis has a feel for it," the running back added. "He seems to know just how far he can go and when he has to get rid of the ball. There is nobody else like him."

There very likely hasn't been anyone else either who has been involved in the kinds of trades Tarkenton has been peddled in.

The first came in 1967, after he had served a six-year tenure with Minnesota, and followed a letter of resignation he wrote to Norm Van Brocklin and Van Brocklin's own resignation from the Vikings' coaching position.

The letter culminated a growing difference of opinion between the quarterback and the coach and said in part:

"Because of the events of the past few months and my feelings toward a number of things, it is impossible for me to return to the Vikings with a clear and open mind. As you know I have tried to subdue these feelings and erase them from my mind, but it has been impossible."

Jim Finks, the general manager, who himself had been an NFL quarterback, tried to convince Fran to remain in Minnesota, but the strong-willed quarterback remained firm and he soon became a New York Giant. He was, of course, an immediate hit in New York, and both his image and his off-fiield business empire flourished. But after four years with the Giants, it became apparent that his run wouldn't last forever, not even until he retired.

The incident that created an irreparable wedge between Tarkenton and the Giants occurred during their contract negotiations prior to the 1971 season. The sticking point in Tarkenton's discussions with Wellington Mara, the Giants' owner and their biggest fan, was a request for a hefty loan instead of the routine salary arrangement. When they couldn't reach an agreement, Tarkenton left the Giants just before they were to play an exhibition game in Houston.

"I wasn't going to hang around and I wasn't going to play without a contract so I figured it was better for everyone if I left," explained Tarkenton, who returned a few days later and signed his contract.

But Mara and the rest of the Giants felt their quarterback and team leader had walked out on them, and the rapport between them never was the same. That helped pave the way for the quarterback's return to Minnesota.

The trade came about after Tarkenton and Mara discussed the Giants' future and what it would take to turn them into a winner. They agreed a large rebuilding job was necessary and that anyone could be traded, including Tarkenton. At that point, Fran told Mara that if he were traded, he'd prefer to go to a contending team, namely, Baltimore, Kansas City, Minnesota, Oakland or Washington.

Mara contacted Finks in Minnesota, and after about a month of negotiations, Tarkenton was on his way back.

"The day I heard the news I felt ten years younger," Tarkenton said. "This is what I have wanted. I left the Vikings just when they were beginning to make noise. I watched those guys develop and learn and then I left and they began winning. It kind of hurt because I have many good friends on the team and I kept in touch while I was playing in New York."

In going to the Vikings, Tarkenton knew he would be faced with a type of pressure he never had experienced before. "What I have to do is win right away," he acknowledged. "I have a lot to prove and it's a different kind of pressure. Now I'm expected to win. That's never happened to me before."

Tarkenton of course felt he could live up to everyone's expectations of him and he immediately took command of the Viking offense. His arrival brought instant improvement to the Minnesota scoring punch.

It happened in the Vikings' first exhibition game, in fact, on the very first kickoff in the first game. Clint Jones took the kick on the one-yard line and raced 99 yards for a touchdown. Standing on the sideline, Tarkenton turned to Bud Grant, the Minnesota coach, and said, "I told you I'd help your offense."

Unfortunately, the Vikings went downhill after that and fell well short of their Super Bowl goal. But Tarkenton was home again and there would be more opportunities to achieve their mutual ambition. Furthermore, at least the Viking offense was a little more stable than it was in the early expansion years. There was the game, for example, where the Vikings were losing to Green Bay, 23–21, there was less than a minute to play and they had the ball near their own goal line with fourth-and-28. There was, of course, no way for Tarkenton to pull this one out. But he was going to try.

"Everybody out for a pass," he ordered in the huddle. "Ends turn and hook upfield, backs try to go long and get free. I'm just gonna scramble until I spot somebody open."

Taking the ball, Tarkenton did exactly that. He scrambled until he had to pass or lie down and surrender. Finally, he lofted a long, high pass in the general direction of a purple shirt and somehow the ball was caught. It wasn't long enough for a touchdown, but with eighteen seconds to play, Fred Cox kicked a field goal that gave the Vikings a 24–23 victory.

It was an improvised play, but it worked. These days, Tarkenton wouldn't mind improvising a championship that worked.

John Unitas

It was like a love affair shattered by deceit and mistrust. It was a divorce ending in a hair-pulling, screaming, kicking confrontaton. It was a family ripped apart by a fierce fight over the family fortune. It was a clash so bitter that John Unitas could say publicly to Gary Huff, a top-notch quarterback, "As you prepare for the draft, Gary, there is only one thing I can say to you. Don't get picked by Baltimore."

For a man who so rarely showed any emotion, no matter what the situation, no matter what the pressure, the acrimony with which Unitas spoke that January evening in 1973 clearly indicated how serious had been the wound inflicted by the action of the new leadership of the Baltimore Colts.

To say John Unitas and the Baltimore Colts had been like saying Babe Ruth and Yankee Stadium, Abbott and Costello, Liz Taylor and Richard Burton. John Unitas was the Baltimore Colts and the Baltimore Colts were John Unitas. The John Unitas Colts.

And then Carroll Rosenbloom traded the Colts for the Los Angeles Rams in the strangest deal ever made in the National Football League. "It was," said one Colt, "like going from a godfather to a stepfather."

Robert Irsay, a Chicago businessman, was the new owner of the Colts in 1972 and he entrusted the operation of the club to Joe Thomas, the man whom had brought him and Rosenbloom together and the man who had helped build two expansion teams, Minnesota and Miami, into champions. Immediately, the atmosphere surrounding the Colts changed. Whereas Rosenbloom had been a paternalistic man who constantly inquired about his players' welfare and frequently insured their healthy financial status, the new people remained aloof, establishing a clear-cut employer-employee relationship. As far as the Colt players were concerned, they could have been working for General Motors.

"A lot of things happened that upset an awful lot of the players," Unitas says. "For example, we were in training camp for four or five weeks before any of the players knew who Joe Thomas or Bob Irsay was. They never even made it a point to come down and say hello to the players and introduce themselves. They probably had reasons for it, but it just didn't sit well with the players."

Unitas most likely could have ignored that kind of behavior; he never was one who needed the insincere glad-handing, back-slapping type of acknowledgment of his existence. If an owner, such as Carrol Rosenbloom, sincerely was interested in him and concerned about him, fine. Phoney friends need not bother. But the absence of action by Irsay and Thomas wasn't the only behavior that affected the greatest quarterback who ever played the game. It was a concrete move that Thomas made early in the 1972 season that created a permanent schism between Unitas and the Colts.

It happened at about three o'clock of the Monday afternoon following the Colts' fifth game, a 21–0 loss to Dallas.

"I was at the stadium in the whirlpool," Unitas relates, "and Thomas called and told me they had just made a coaching change. I said, yeah, I heard about it. And then he said, 'Well, we're going with younger fellows and that means that Marty's going to be playing [Marty Domres, Baltimore's young quarterback], but I don't want you to take this as a slap in the face.' Hell, what was it but a slap in the face?

"I wasn't very happy about it. I thought I was having a good season and I didn't think I was the cause of us losing the football games because I was doing everything I could possibly do in order to win them. I was moving the team up and down the field, but in a couple of instances we didn't score enough points. Still, I was having a good year and playing better than I probably had in the last three years. I was throwing the ball as well, if not better, than the last three years.

"But the word I got later was that Thomas wanted me replaced after the New York Jet game [second of the season] and the coach [Don McCafferty] refused to do it. He said it wasn't my fault, that the fact that we weren't winning the games was a lot of people's fault. Then after the San Diego game, the owner called the coach during the middle of the week and said he wanted me replaced. Mac said no; he refused to do it for the same reason he gave before. Then the following Monday he was replaced and I was replaced.

"I think they went ahead and made the change too soon. We still could have been in the race if we beat New York the second time and then came back and beat Miami. If I had been playing, we possibly had a chance to do that and then we would have been in the race. But if we lost both those games, as we did, then we were definitely out of the race. That was the time for him to move Domres in, but not before we're out of the race. I think he pulled the string too fast and he threw the towel in."

There was no way Thomas could defend the move to the incensed football populace of Baltimore. They had lived with and loved Unitas for seventeen seasons, ever since he replaced George Shaw in the fourth game of the 1956 season when Shaw broke his leg, and while they realized he might not be what he used to be, gods and heroes require better treatment than a phone call and a seat on the bench.

"He's the Babe Ruth of pro football," acknowledged Thomas, who copied the Yankees' trade of Ruth to the Boston Braves by shipping Unitas to San Diego. "It's tough. If I had waited until the end of the season to make a change, no one would have criticized me. But we would have lost another year in rebuilding."

While the Colts were rebuilding, mid-season style, with Domres, an Ivy Leaguer from Columbia by way of the San Diego Chargers, Unitas was sitting, playing only when Domres was hurt. Those moments were brief. The game against San Francisco, for instance, when Unitas left the bench for one play, an ignominious moment when he was dumped for a 21-yard loss and fumbled the ball away. Or the last pass he threw as a Colt, a pass against Miami in the final game of the 1972 season that was intercepted by Doug Swift, a linebacker who was barely removed from kindergarten when Unitas threw his first pro pass.

That first pass, curiously, also was intercepted (by J. C. Caroline of the Chicago Bears), but in between there were 2,796 passes that were completed for 39,768 yards and 287 touchdowns, all pro football records that stand as a tribute to the man whose exit from the Colts was as lionish as his entry into pro football was lambish.

The story is as well known as Tom Sawyer. Drafted in the ninth round by the Pittsburgh Steelers in 1955, Unitas never even played in an exhibition game before he was cut by his hometown team. Then after playing that season for the semi-pro Bloomfield Rams in Pittsburgh for six dollars a game, he was invited to a Baltimore tryout camp by General Manager Don Kellett in an eighty-five-cent phone call and went on from there, under Coach Weeb Ewbank, to become the premier quarterback of the first fifty years of NFL play.

Unitas, a crew-cut, unsmiling human machine, led the Colts to league and conference championships and established a flock of passing records while doing it, including one of the most awesome marks in the book—a string of forty-seven consecutive games from December 9, 1956, through December 4, 1960, in which he threw at least one touchdown pass a game. Records, however, don't take up any space in Unitas's mind.

"I don't even know what records I hold," he said not long ago. "I don't look at records and don't even think about them. The only record I'm interested in is win or lose. Winning football games, that's all."

Indeed, Unitas won a lot of football games while he was at Baltimore, and none was more impressive than the 14–3 victory he engineered over Miami toward the end of the 1971 season, when he was considered by some critics to be a washed-up 38-year-old hanger-on.

Playing against a team that was to play in the Super Bowl a month later, Unitas masterfully directed two long touchdown drives that were to football what the Mona Lisa is to art. The first drive, in the first quarter, covered 81 yards and consumed 18 plays and 9 minutes, 53 seconds; the second, in the second quarter, traveled 87 yards and lasted 16 plays and 9 minutes, 26 seconds. Unitas did it by picking apart the Dolphins' reputed zone defense with short passes and sure runs.

"You don't expect the quarterback to be reading you like that," said Nick Buoniconti, the Miami middle linebacker who was as powerless to stop the Unitas onslaught as any other member of the defense. "A quarterback usually looks at the strong safety and strong side linebacker for his keys. But with Unitas, its scary. He seems to know what you're going to do before you do."

The drives epitomized Unitas's art of play-calling, an ability he possesses even though his arm might not be what it once was. He calls plays

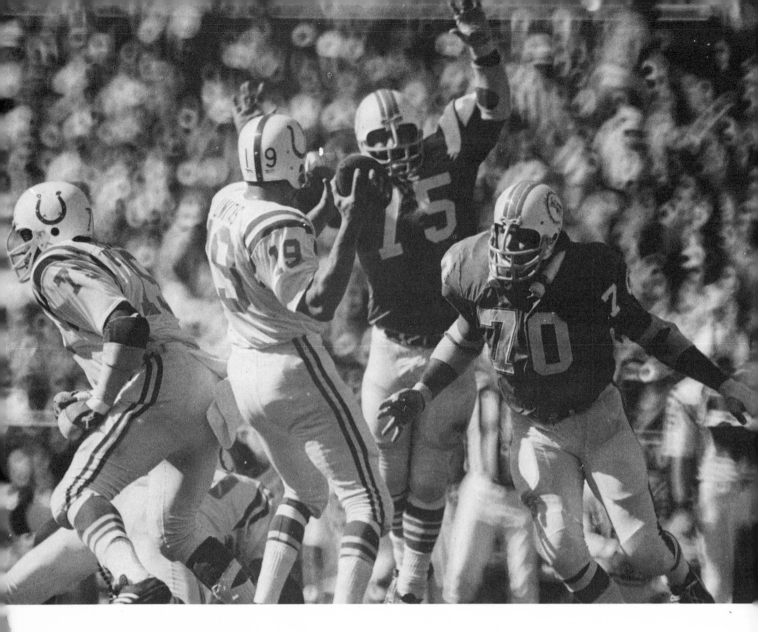

so beautifully they could be put to music or applied to canvas. There is more to long touchdown drives, of course, than calling plays, but Unitas has that, too.

"You have to have the complete confidence of your offensive men and there has to be a complete dedication on everybody's part to know what you're trying to," he says.

When Unitas stood in the Colt huddle or behind the Colt center, there was no doubt that he had that confidence and dedication. He had clearly earned it from his teammates. One illustration will suffice.

The Colts were playing the Chicago Bears in a game in 1970 and they and Unitas were not having too much success. Neither was Eddie Hinton, a young receiver. Hinton already had dropped three passes that he should have caught, but now in a crucial fourth-and-2 situation, Unitas threw to him again, a pass to the sideline that Hinton leaped high for and

grabbed at the one-yard line. The Colts went on from there to overcome a 17–0 deficit and win, 21–20.

"I was so miserable in that game," Hinton recalls. "I couldn't hold anything and I couldn't even say I'm sorry. I never thought he would come to me on that fourth down pass, but he did and nobody but God and myself will ever know what that did for me. I wanted to cry. I wanted to rush up to him and throw my arms around his neck and just say, 'I love you.'"

Two years later, Hinton was involved in a play for which Unitas, if he were prone to such emotions, could have said, "I love you." This time the Colts were playing their final home game of the season, against Buffalo, and it was obvious Unitas never again would trot onto the Memorial Stadium field wearing the blue and white uniform with the horseshoe-decorated helmet.

Earlier in the week, John Sandusky, the Colts' interim coach, was discussing the possibility of letting Unitas play for a few minutes so his loyal fans could properly wish him farewell. "I wouldn't ask John to make a token appearance," Sandusky said. "If I did, he would tell me what I could do with it and I couldn't blame him."

But Sandusky didn't have to ask Unitas anything. When Domres injured his knee in the fourth quarter, the coach simply told Unitas to get in there. Just minutes before, a plane had passed over the stadium pulling a banner which said, "Unitas we stand," and the crowd roared. Now when their hero ran onto the field, they roared again and he was to give them cause for one more standing ovation.

After calling a running play and a pass to Lydell Mitchell, Unitas called an "A cut" pass to Hinton, a medium length toss to the right sideline. "It's nothing fancy," Hinton says, "but after I caught it, all I was thinking was touchdown, touchdown. Once I started down the sideline, Maurice Tyler [the Bills' defensive back] was running with me, but I wasn't about to let him stop me. I just wanted to get in the end zone. I didn't care how. And then when I crossed the goal line I suddenly realized what really happened. It was a very emotional moment and suddenly I felt great because I was part of the moment."

It would have been fitting, of course, for Unitas to have walked off the field after that 63-yard touchdown pass play, never to return to a huddle. But that isn't Unitas. Despite the pleadings of those people who have wanted him to retire for the past few years because they want him to go out on top, the aging but irrepressible quarterback refuses to quit until he feels he no longer can call the plays and make them work. He frequently has said it doesn't matter to him how he leaves the game, on top or tumbling toward the bottom.

"Why should it matter?" he says. "I'm not concerned about my image or reputation. The only thing to be concerned about is playing football. It's something I enjoy doing and something I get paid very well for doing. You always try to make every season a winning season, but whether or not you go out as a winner or whether your last season is a losing season, it really doesn't make that much difference. And as far as Baltimore is concerned, they took my last year there away from me without even discussing it or talking to me about it."